QUILT
THE BELOVED COUNTRY

BY JENNY WILLIAMSON AND PAT PARKER

"THANK YOUS" FOR OUR BOOK

There are a number of people without whose help this book would not have come to fruition. We would like them all to know that their continued support is much appreciated.

Our warmest thanks to:

Our publisher, Nick Pryke, for his belief in us.

Rob Williamson for hours of his 'free' time so willingly and patiently given in order to achieve the perfect photographs of each and every quilt, as well as their inspirations.

Shelley Williamson for the outstanding design and layout of our book.

Our quilting friends, for allowing us to include their wonderful African quilts. They are Carolyn Kode, Pat Perry, Shirley Prakke, Terry Pryke, Paul Schutte and Carol Smith.

Finally, the Southern Stars Quilting Group, both past and present, all of whom have shared our passion for quilting over many years.

First published in 2008 by Wild Dog Press P.O. Box 1649, Highlands North, 2037, South Africa.

This edition published by American Quilter's Society. P.O. Box 3290, Paducah, KY 42002-3290. www.AmericanQuilter.com

ISBN 978-1-57432-989-6

Copyright © Jenny Williamson and Pat Parker

Design by Lime Green Design
Printed in Singapore by Tien Wah Press 2008

American Quilter's Society
Located in Paducah, Kentucky, the American Quilter's Society (AQS) is dedicated to promoting the accomplishments of today's quilters. Through its publications and events, AQS strives to honor today's quiltmakers and their work and to inspire future creativity and innovation in quiltmaking.

CONTENTS

SOUL SISTERS

The craft of African quilting is a beautifully textured and vibrant art form that bears testimony to the rich and complex nature of the African continent. In this, their third book, doyennes of the discipline Pat Parker and Jenny Williamson, delve deeper into what it is that sets this relatively new style quilting apart from the more well-established American and European styles that have dominated quilting circles for hundreds of years.

For twenty-five years these 'soul sisters' have been patient teachers and dedicated practitioners of the art of quilting. They are so passionate about their craft, that they insist, "the only difference between us and an artist is that we use fabrics, not paints!".

They also reveal that, "much to our poor husbands' chagrin, we don't do buttons or mending. It's just too boring! We'd far rather be thinking about, or even better, actually creating a new quilt. We're always thinking of new ideas and absorbing sights, sounds, colors and textures from our surroundings, with a view to producing our next quilt. We're mad about quilts, because they bring us such joy!"

And it's no wonder, when you consider that the quilts they produce are a world away from an assortment of patches roughly sewn together. The quilts they craft and have presented in this book, are carefully thought out patterns of beautifully colored and textured materials. They take hours to conceptualise and many, many months to put together, in carefully composed patterns that delight the eye and bring their final surroundings to life.

These quilts are also once off masterpieces that, for the most part have been painstakingly hand stitched – some in their entirety. It's well worth the effort though, when you consider that the end product is an artwork that can be hung in a variety of locations, from boardrooms to living rooms.

This kind of standard is only possible, however, because whichever way you look at it, these 'soul sisters' have stitching in their blood. This has allowed them to remain as passionate and dedicated to their craft as they were when they first took up the discipline over 30 years ago.

Since then they have played a pioneering role in shaping a unique genre of African quilting, having conducted basic, intermediate and advanced courses in piecing, appliqué, quilting and embroidery. They have also taught courses at the South African National Quilt Festivals since 1988, as well as the International Quilt Festivals held in Houston and Paducah in the U.S.A. and Harrogate in the U.K.

Where it all began...

Looking back to the inception of their love affair with the African style of quilting, Pat and Jenny reveal that the idea for their adopting a more African-inspired approach to quilting, came about in 1991 when a fellow quilter from the US asked: "Where are the quilts from Africa?"

"We suddenly realised that there was very little quilting that reflected the rich colour and vibrancy of African culture and did justice to the rhythm and pace of our beautiful continent," says Jenny.

This led to their creating their first 'African style' quilt 'Leap Year in the Lowveld', beautifully presented in a fresh new African style. This award-winning quilt has subsequently been exhibited worldwide.

It also led to their first book being published in 1998 to great acclaim, followed by yet another very successful book in 2004. They have since been invited to numerous international quilting shows, which have seen them visiting the quilting capitals of the world including the US on two occasions, as well as the UK, Canada and quite surprisingly Japan, where quilting is incredibly popular.

At these events they have displayed their unique collection of African inspired quilts with great success, generating incredible interest from exhibition goers from across the globe who, more often than not, are exposed to the vibrancy of African quilting style for the first time.

In living color

Jenny and Pat say that one of the biggest draw cards at these events, and the key element that distinguishes the African style of quilting from more muted, conservative traditional styles of quilting, is its incredible use of vibrant, vivid color.

"We are not big fans of beige and cream because we have always loved color since we were children. We have lived with color our entire lives. Our Mother made beautifully bright clothes and our grandmother did costume sewing, so you could say that color is in our blood!" explains Pat.

As a result, the quilts they produce are not a hodgepodge of off-cuts or scraps. Pat and Jenny spend many hours scouring the markets and downtown Johannesburg, searching for just the right mix of colorful fabrics that are the key differentiators of the African style of quilting, with which they have become synonymous.

Another key feature of the local style of quilting is the use of images drawn from its vibrant flora and fauna, the faces of its people and by Jenny and Pat, simply drinking in their surroundings every day. Unlike many people, however, these 'soul sisters' possess an uncanny ability for translating these visions of Africa into beautiful one-of-a-kind quilts!

We hope you enjoy your journey through their third African quilting odyssey – a beautiful palette of textures, colors and patterns that continue to make African quilting a joy to behold!

Text by Luise Alleman of Mediaink

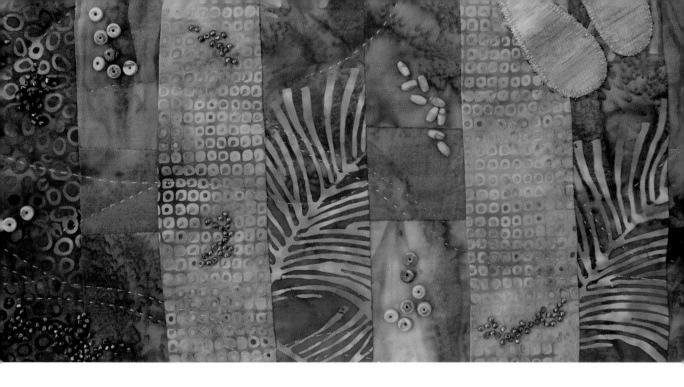

SHALL WE BEGIN

Many of you who know our books will see that we have repeated the instructions for a few of the quilts that were included in 'Quilts on Safari'. The reason for this is that 'Quilts on Safari' is now out of print and we are constantly being asked for the instructions for some of the quilts. We trust, however, that there will also be more than enough new work for you to use and enjoy.

Because the fundamentals of making African quilts do not change and what we have said before is still as relevant as ever, we ask you to read the following guidelines before beginning a quilt from our book. They should help you to understand better our methods of instruction.

Choice of Fabrics

As far as the choice of fabrics is concerned, this is a golden opportunity to leave your 'comfort zone'.

Whether it be artwork or clothing, the people of Africa choose an unpredictable variety of vibrant and seemingly clashing colors. Do not forget this when planning a quilt.

Audition the fabrics, choosing the ones which are most suitable for huts, trees, people, animals, birds, etc. Then move the fabrics around until the result is most successful.

Do not be too inhibited. The greater the variety introduced, the more successful the end result. Introduce some startling 'uglies'. Don't choose fabrics that look too realistic – naivety looks great! Hand dyed fabrics are good – particularly for backgrounds.

We recommend 100% cotton for hand appliqué. When doing machine appliqué, however, use whatever fabric gives the desired effect, whether it be cotton blends, satin, wool, silk, organza, netting, etc.

We are assuming that all fabric is 45" (115cm) wide. If this is not the case

the given quantities will need to be adjusted. (More fabric needed if it is narrower and less if it is wider.)

Hand Appliqué

It is advisable to make a tracing of the motifs you intend to appliqué. Hold this over your fabric and then place your pieces under the tracing in the correct position. If you have a number of pieces to appliqué, give each piece a different number and mark your vylene with the same number.

Due to the fact that it is often difficult to remove various marking pens and pencils, we prefer to use a method by which we do not have to mark the fabric at all.

Use a fine ball-point pen to trace the design onto iron-on vylene. We like to use a vylene that is thin and pliable, with bonding only on one side.

When tracing the design onto the vylene, always have the bonded side down. Cut vylene along the marked lines. (No seam allowance). Position the vylene onto the fabric as desired. The grain of the fabric is not important, rather iron the vylene onto the fabric to obtain the best effect.

Iron the vylene lightly onto the right side of the fabric, placing a plain white sheet of paper between the iron and the work. (Should you inadvertently iron onto the wrong side of the vylene, only the vylene and paper will have to be replaced, not the iron!)

Use a dry iron, no steam, but do not allow it to be too hot (e.g. wool setting or cooler, depending upon your iron), otherwise the bonding will melt and cause the vylene to adhere too firmly to the fabric. It is always advisable to test on a scrap before commencing.

After vylene has been ironed in place, cut a seam allowance of between ⅛" (3mm) and ¼" (6mm).

Working on a flat surface, pin appliqué pieces to base. We find the tiny appliqué pins indispensable, as the long ones tend to get in the way.

We sew with either an Appliqué or Crewel (Embroidery) needle (Size 9 or 10), but we suggest that whatever needle is correct for you is acceptable. If you have young eyes and dainty fingers by all means use a 12!

Match the thread as closely as possible to the color of the piece being appliquéd. If the match is not perfect always go for a darker rather than a lighter thread.

Sew small blind hemming stitches about $\frac{1}{8}$" (3mm) apart. Pull thread firmly upwards towards you as you go.

Concave curves need to be clipped to release the tension.

Remove vylene as each piece is applied.

Machine Appliqué

It is advisable to make a tracing of the motifs you intend to appliqué. Hold this over your fabric and then place your pieces under the tracing in the correct position. If you have a number of pieces to appliqué, give each piece a different number and mark your vylene with the same number.

As in hand appliqué, use a fine ball-point pen to trace the design onto the vylene. When tracing the design onto the vylene always have the bonded side up, and when ironing the vylene onto the fabric always have the bonded side down. Iron this onto the wrong side of the fabric.

Do not worry about the grain, rather iron the vylene onto the fabric to obtain the best effect. Use a dry iron, but do not allow it to be too hot. Place a sheet of clean white paper between the iron and the work.

Use a zig-zag machine with a suitable foot (one which has no metal or plastic between the toes to block your view as you sew).

When doing machine appliqué fibre deposits build up very quickly around the bobbin area, so it is necessary to clean and oil your machine regularly. Make sure that the needle is sharp, as a blunt needle is the main cause of irregular stitching (we like to use a 70/10 or 80/12 needle).

Always put a sheet of magazine paper underneath your work when machining i.e. between your work and the feed dog. This will act as a stabilizer and prevent the work from puckering. When stitching is complete remember to remove the paper from the back of the work! Pull threads to the back of your work and cut off as you go.

For satin stitch your stitches should be close enough to form a solid line, but not be so close that they bunch up and jam the machine. (If you let go of the fabric when sewing, the feed dog should carry the fabric through without a problem).

For a more contemporary look alter your stitch lengths and widths until you get the desired effect.

You may even wish to leave the raw edges and sew with a straight stitch.

Try using different threads. This is an area that can be such a lot of fun!

Remember that appliqué is a means of stitching one fabric to another. How it is done is not important as long as the end result is successful. This is where one can be really creative!

Anyone can do appliqué work. It is a medium that can be both rewarding and stimulating.

Piecing

Whether you are doing hand or machine piecing, it is imperative to work accurately. We use a $^1/4$" (10mm) seam allowance throughout.

If your seams are not exactly $^1/4$" (10mm) you will need to adjust our given measurements. We suggest that you sew 3 small squares together. Cut them $2^1/2$" x $2^1/2$" (70mm x 70mm). When they are stitched they should measure $6^1/2$" (170mm) from the left to the right hand edges. If they do not, adjust your seam allowance until they do.

Before cutting borders please measure your quilt top across the middle for both length and width. If your size is slightly different from the sizes given, you will need to adjust your sizes accordingly. For example: the given width measurement is $40^1/2$" (103cm) and your quilt top measures $41^1/2$" (105cm) – difference 1" (2 cm) you will need to add 1" (2cm) to the given size. The same applies to your length measurement.

When using the piecing templates, make as given then add $^1/4$" (10mm) seam allowance when cutting fabric. Your work will be more accurate if you do this.

The arrow on the templates indicates the direction of the grain of the fabric.

Pressing

Pressing means literally what it says – press the iron gently onto the fabric. If you push too hard you will stretch the fabric.

Press the seams as you go.

Do not open the seams as it weakens them. Wherever possible press the seams towards the darkest fabric.

Press seams away from where you wish to quilt.

Signing Your Quilts

Make sure you personalize your quilts. Always sign and date your quilts – either on the front or back. Include any other information that you feel is relevant e.g. maybe the name of the person or the occasion for which the quilt has been made.

QUILT GALLERY

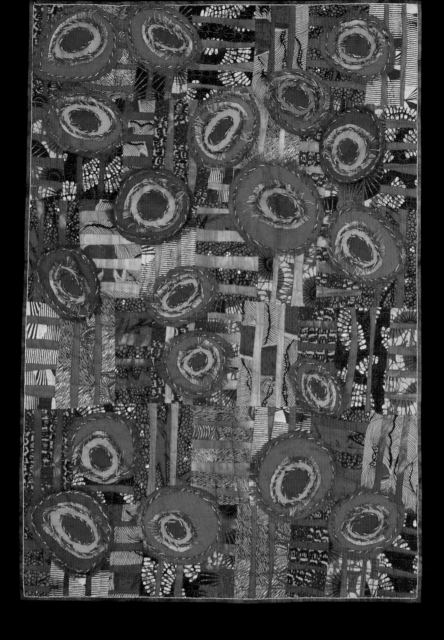

DESERT FLOWERS – Pat Parker

A nostalgic reminder of the vibrant vygies seen growing on the rocks in the Western Cape.

INTSIZWA AND INTOMBI – Carol Smith
(Young Man and Young Woman)

Could any quilts be more African?

CELEBRATION – Carol Smith

This quilt reflects the incredible rhythms of Africa.

PERMUTATION – Pat Perry

Based on a pattern used to decorate some of the clay houses in the Northern Limpopo Province where Tsonga and Pedi people lived together.

WE BELIEVE IN ANGELS – Jenny Williamson and Pat Parker

No snow for us at Christmas-time –
so we used our hottest colors to celebrate a
sweltering festive day.

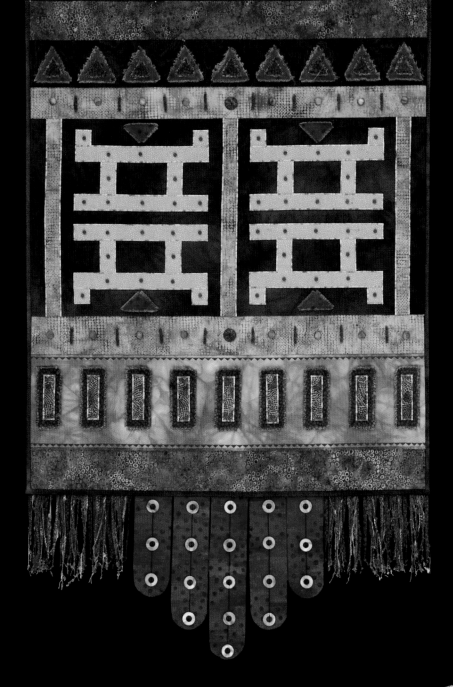

NDEBELE APRON – Jenny Williamson

I was inspired by the Ndebele aprons.

DASHING TO DURBAN – Jenny Williamson and Pat Parker

We made this "fun" quilt to celebrate the various journeys being made by so many quilters to the National Quilt Festival.

VILLAGE PEOPLE – Jenny Williamson and Pat Parker

Catching up with the local gossip on washday.

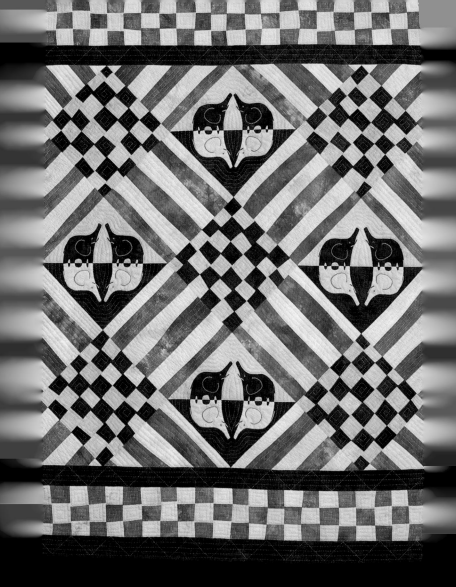

— Pat Parker

...espect for these 'gentle giants' whose
...ay be threatened by the continual
...f man on our continent.

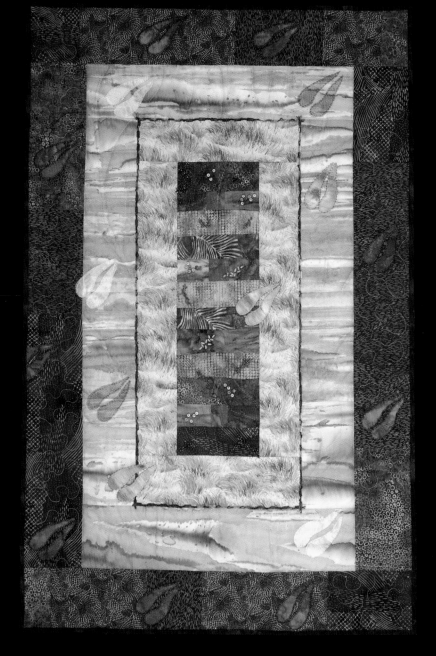

KALAHARI DAWN – Jenny Williamson

A recent visit inspired me to make a quilt capturing the moods, colors, grasses, dunes and gemsbok footprints in the sand.

LIBERTY IN AFRICA – Jenny Williamson

I thought it was time for "Liberty of London" to visit Africa!

PSAMMOBATES GEOMETRICUS – Shirley Prakke

This little tortoise is one of the rarest
reptiles in the world, on the edge of extinction,
with a highly decorative shell.

INCANTATION ON IMMORTALITY – Terry Pryke

I would like to thank artist, David Smuts,
for allowing me to give a quilter's
interpretation of his painting.

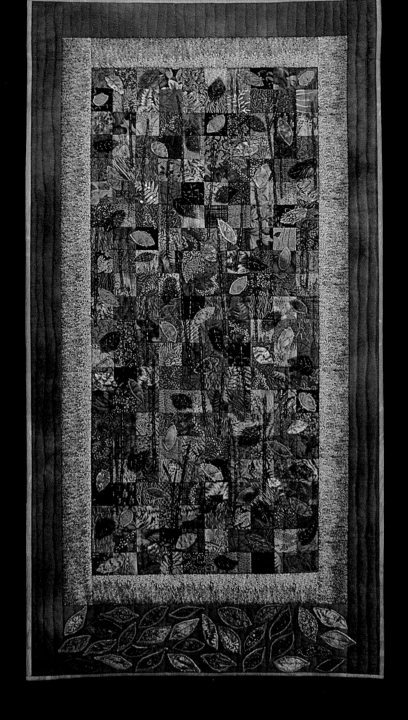

YOU CAN'T SEE THE WOODS FOR THE LEAVES
– Jenny Williamson

Our forests are magical – they must be preserved.

BRILLIANT BAOBAB – Carolyn Kode

The magnificent baobab is unmistakable because of its massive trunk
and sparse, spreading crown.

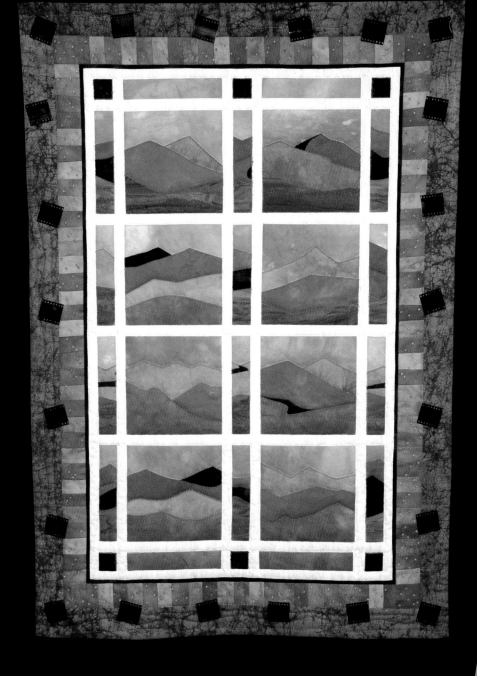

SHIFTING SANDS – Jenny Williamson

After attending a photographic workshop at Sossusvlei,
I was inspired to make a dune quilt.

TIME ORIENTATIONS: AFRO-CENTRIC
VERSUS EURO-CENTRIC – Paul Schutte

The surface is a visual metaphor of the 'crossing' of the two time orientations when living in a multi-cultured South Africa. The textile surface suggests that harmony is possible with accommodation and tolerance when love (symbolized by the crosses) is present.

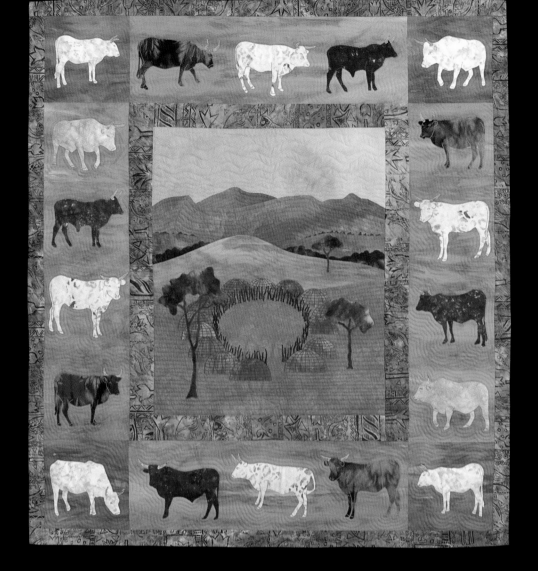

ZULU KINGDOM – Jenny Williamson and Pat Parker

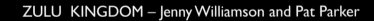

The Nguni cattle are an integral part of the economic, political, social and spiritual well-being of the Zulu nation.

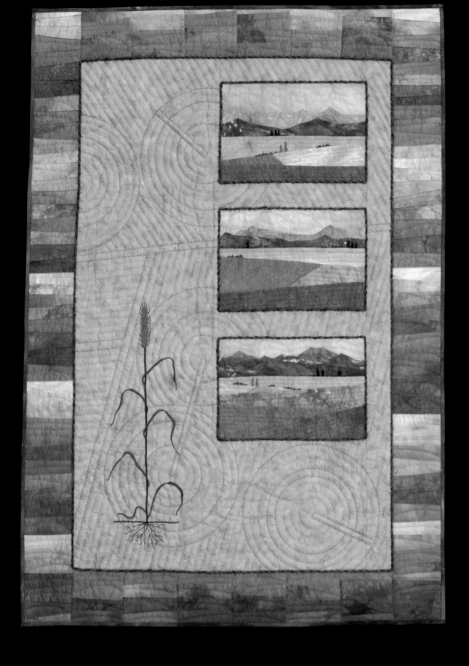

CIRCLES IN THE SAND – Pat Parker

I am always fascinated by the near perfect circles seen in the wheat fields of the Free State after harvest time.

QUILTS TO MAKE

AFRICAN ALPHABET – Jenny Williamson and Pat Parker

53" x 63" (132cm x 157cm)

AFRICAN ALPHABET

These were the images that came to mind when we decided to make an African alphabet quilt. Should you wish to do so, feel free to make changes.

Techniques

May be appliquéd and quilted either by hand or machine. Should be machine pieced.

Block Size

8"x 8" (20cm x 20cm)

Materials

Background fabric	2 yd	(2m)
Fabric for letters, sashing squares & binding.	1 $\frac{1}{2}$ yd	(1.5m)
Batting	59"x 69"	(147cm x 172cm)
Backing	59"x 69"	(147cm x 172cm)

A selection of printed fabrics suitable for appliqué motifs and sashing strips. The sizes for the sashing strips are 18" x 4$\frac{1}{2}$" (460mm x 130mm). The more the merrier!

Method

The appliqué shapes need to be enlarged thus:

Take the letter 'A' and have it enlarged until it measures the size given on diagram. Then have all letters and shapes increased by the same percentage.

Using background fabric cut 28 squares 8$\frac{1}{2}$"x 8$\frac{1}{2}$" (220cm x 220cm)

Appliqué all squares.

Now make the lengths for sashing strips. You need to have 17 pairs of fabric 18"x 4$\frac{1}{2}$" (460mm x 130mm). Each pair will give you 4 sashing strips. You may repeat some of the fabrics, but your quilt will look more exciting if you choose different fabrics for each pair.

Place these fabrics together in pairs so that the first fabric is directly on top of the second with RIGHT SIDES FACING UPWARDS.

Using rotary cutter make a curved cut lengthwise on each pair. (Do not make curves too severe or the stitching will be difficult).

Now take TOP left fabric and BOTTOM right fabric.

With right sides facing sew together. Press seam allowance to one side.

Take BOTTOM left fabric and TOP right fabric. With right sides facing sew together. Press seam allowance to one side.

Repeat this procedure until all 17 pairs have been sewn.

Now from these pieced lengths cut 67 sashing strips 8$\frac{1}{2}$"x 2$\frac{1}{2}$" (220mm x 70mm).

Using same fabric as used for letters cut 44 sashing squares 2$\frac{1}{2}$" x 2$\frac{1}{2}$" (70mm x 70mm).

Join quilt top as follows:

Using photograph as guide, make 6 rows made up of 6 sashing squares and 5 sashing strips and 1 row with 4 sashing squares and 3 sashing strips.

Then make 5 rows with 5 background squares and 6 sashing strips and 1 row with 3 background squares and 4 sashing strips. (You will have 13 rows).

Join first 11 rows to form section (1) and last 2 rows to form section (2).

Keep these sections separate – this is to make the binding easier.

Now do the quilting.

Bind section (1) on all sides. Bind section (2) at base and on the two sides – not on the top.

Place section (2) behind section (1) in correct position and using small blind hemming stitches hand sew this to the base of section (1).

Cut a piece of binding fabric 1" (30mm) longer than raw edge of section (2) x 1" (30mm). Turn in $\frac{1}{4}$" (8mm) on all sides and cover raw edges on back of quilt.

SECTION 1

A	B	C	D	E
F	G	H	I	J
K	L	M	N	O
P	Q	R	S	T
U	V	W	X	Y

SECTION 2

!	Z	!

2¹/₂" (65mm)

ALOE

BAOBAB

C CROCODILE

D DRUM

E ELEPHANT

F 1 2 3 4 5 FOOTPRINT

G GIRAFFE

H HUT

IBIS

JACKAL

KUDU

LION

MONKEY

NDEBELE

40

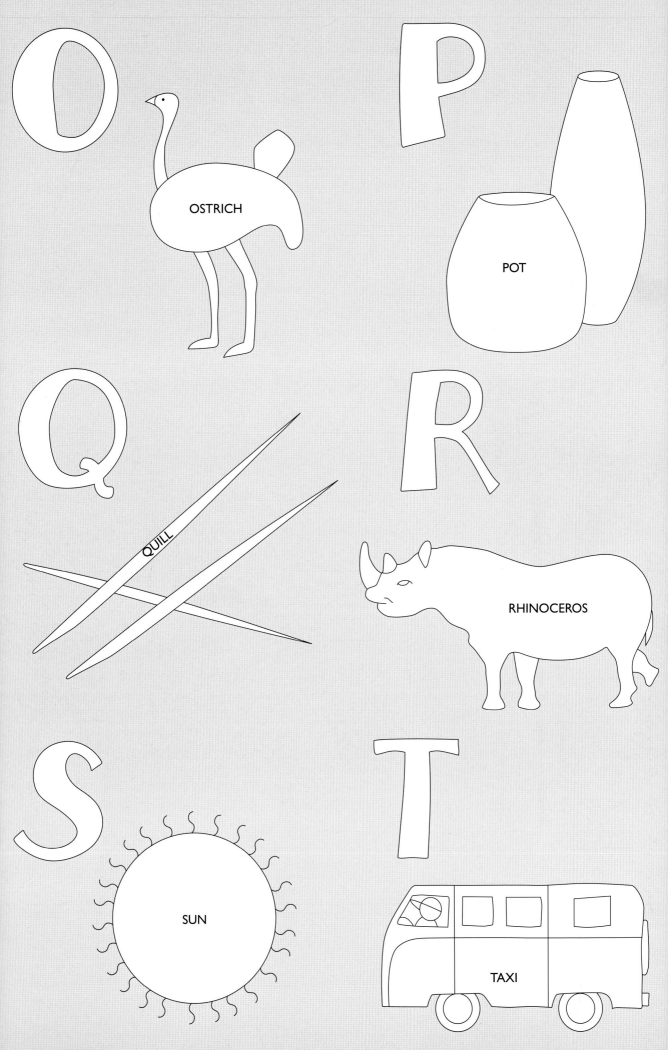

O

OSTRICH

P

POT

Q

QUILL

R

RHINOCEROS

S

SUN

T

TAXI

U UMBRELLA THORN

V VULTURE

W WARTHOG

X XHOSA

Y YELLOW-BILLED STORK

Z ZEBRA

!

AFRICAN ALPHABET

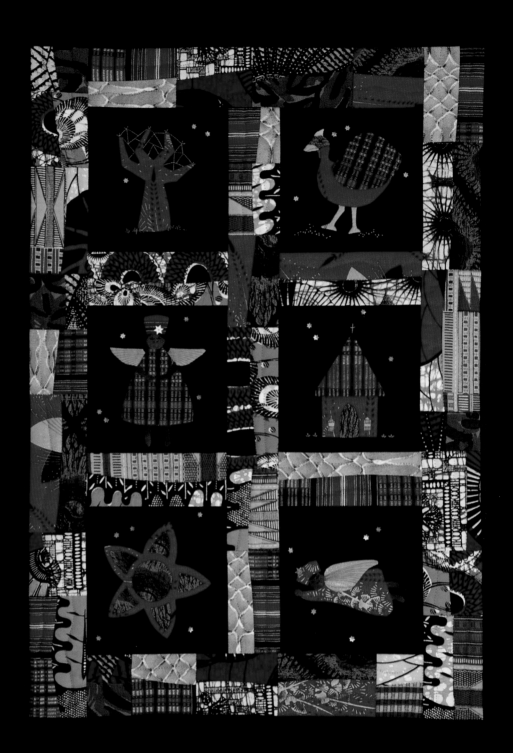

AFRICAN CHRISTMAS – Jenny Williamson and Pat Parker

28" x 40" (68cm x 98cm)

AFRICAN CHRISTMAS

Christmas in Africa is a colorful affair!

Techniques

The appliqué and quilting for this quilt may be done either by hand or machine. The piecing should preferably be done by machine.

Block Size

8"x 8" (200mm x 200mm)

Materials

Black fabric used for background,
squares & binding   1yd   (1m)

An assortment of brightly colored fabrics for appliqué, sashings and borders. The sashings and borders will use 14 pieces of fabric cut 18"x 5" (460mm x 130mm). N.B. You may repeat a fabric, but your quilt will be more successful if all 14 pieces are different.

Backing   34"x 46"   (78cm x 108cm)

Batting   34"x 46"   (78cm x 108cm)

A few gold stars and/or beads for embellishment.

Method

N.B. The appliqué shapes need to be enlarged. Please cut an 8"x 8" (20cm x 20cm) square out of paper. Take upright angel and have her enlarged so that she fits well into your square. There should be a 1" (25mm) gap on all sides. This same percentage of enlargement should then be used for the other shapes.

Cut 6 background squares from black fabric 8½"x 8½"

(220mm x 220mm). Appliqué motifs onto these squares.

Now make strips to be used for sashings and borders as follows:

Cut 1 strip from 14 different fabrics 18"x 5" (460mm x 130mm). Place these fabrics together in pairs (7 pairs) so that the first fabric is directly on top of the second with RIGHT SIDES FACING UPWARDS.

Using rotary cutter make a curved cut lengthwise on each pair. (Do not make curves too severe or the stitching will be difficult).

Now take TOP left hand fabric and BOTTOM right hand fabric. With right sides facing sew together. Press seam allowance to one side.

Take BOTTOM left hand fabric and TOP right hand fabric. With right sides facing sew together. Press seam allowance to one side. Repeat this procedure until all 7 pairs have been sewn.

Place your appliquéd squares on audition board, leaving space for sashings.

Using different strips in each case cut 4 sashings $8^{1}/2$"x $3^{1}/2$" (220mm x 100mm) these will be 7, 8, 9 and 10 on your quilt diagram. Place these on your audition board.

Now cut your remaining strips into smaller lengths and place these randomly down the centre of your quilt and around the borders. At this stage please note that the smaller pieces need not be accurate. When you are satisfied with the placement join the small pieces in each strip together. You can then cut each joined strip to the correct width and length.

Join quilt as follows:

Sew together 1+7+3+9+5. Set aside.

Sew together 2+8+4+10+6. Set aside.

Now cut central strip (11) $30^{1}/2$"x $3^{1}/2$" (780mm x 100mm).

Sew your joined blocks to either side of this central strip.

Cut top and bottom borders (12 and 13) $19^{1}/2$"x 4" (500mm x 120mm). Sew these to quilt.

Cut left and right hand side borders (14 and 15) $38^{1}/2$"x4" (980mm x 120mm). Sew these to quilt.

Now add your embellishments.

Your quilt is ready to be quilted and bound!

Merry Christmas!

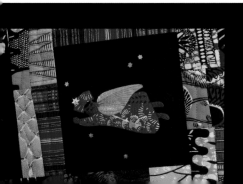

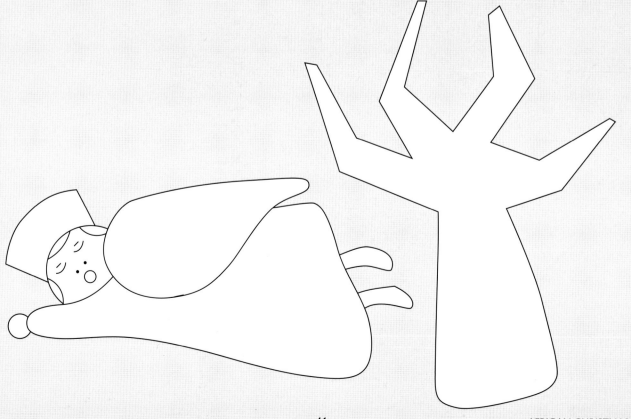

		12		
	1		2	
	7		8	
14	3	11	4	15
	9		10	
	5		6	
		13		

upright angel

ALL A FLUTTER– Jenny Williamson and Pat Parker

58" x 70" (150cm x 180cm)

ALL A FLUTTER

Let your imagination 'fly free'!

Techniques

May be appliquéd, pieced and quilted either by hand or machine.

Block Size

12"x 12" (30cm x 30cm). You will need 12 blocks, 3 across by 4 down.

Materials

Background fabric	3yd	(3m)
Sashing and outside borders	1 1/2 yd	(1.5m)
Selection of fat quarters for butterflies (12 would be good).		
Large appliqué shapes on border	1/2 yd	(0.5m)
Sashing squares and binding	1/2 yd	(0.5m)
Batting	64"x 78"	(165cm x 195cm)
Backing	64"x 78"	(165cm x 195cm)

Method

N.B. The butterflies need to be enlarged. Please cut a 6"x 6" (15cm x 15cm) square out of paper. Take butterfly marked "test for size" and have this enlarged so that it fits well on the diagonal across your paper square. There should be 1/2" (15mm) gap on all sides. This same percentage of enlargement should then be used for the remaining butterflies.

Using background fabric cut:

2 border strips 39 1/2" x 6 1/2" (1000mm x 170mm)(D)

2 border strips 53" x 6 1/2" (1340mm x 170mm)(E)

4 border squares 6$\frac{1}{2}$" x 6 $\frac{1}{2}$" (170mm x 170mm)(F)

12 squares 12$\frac{1}{2}$" x 12$\frac{1}{2}$" (320mm x 320mm)(A)

Using photograph as guide do all appliqué.

Using sashing fabric cut:

31 strips 12$\frac{1}{2}$" x 2" (320mm x 60mm)(B)

Using sashing squares fabric cut:

20 squares 2" x 2" (60mm x 60mm)(C)

Lay background squares 3 across by 4 down.

Working with the top 3 blocks add a sashing strip to the left side of each block and another strip to the right hand edge.

Do the same with the other 3 rows.

Sew 4 sashing squares to three sashing strips, alternating the squares and strips to form a row.

Make another 4 of these rows.

Sew these 9 rows together.

Using sashing fabric cut 8 strips 6 $\frac{1}{2}$" x 2" (170mm x 60mm)(G). Add strip (G) to each end of (D). Sew to top and bottom of quilt. Now join (F) to (G) to (E) to (G) to (F). Sew to left hand side. Repeat for right hand side.

Using border fabric cut:

2 strips 54 $\frac{1}{2}$" x 2" (1380mm x 60mm)(H).

Sew to top and bottom of quilt.

2 strips 71"x 2" (1800mm x 60mm)(J).

Sew to left and right hand sides.

Quilt as desired.

Bind with same fabric used for sashing squares.

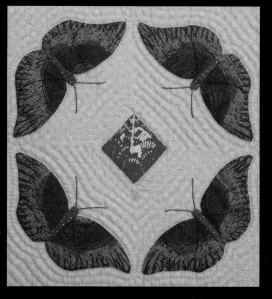

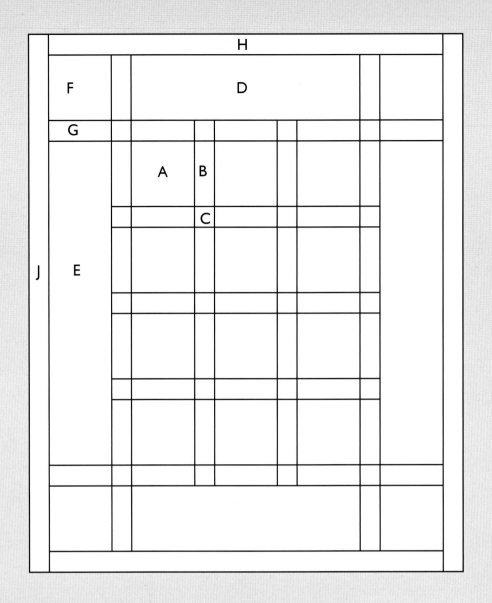

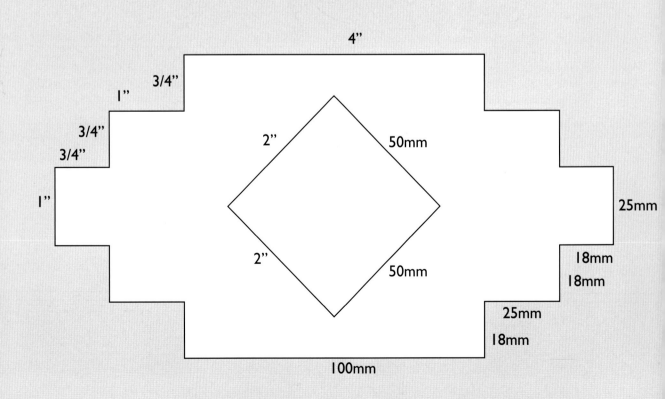

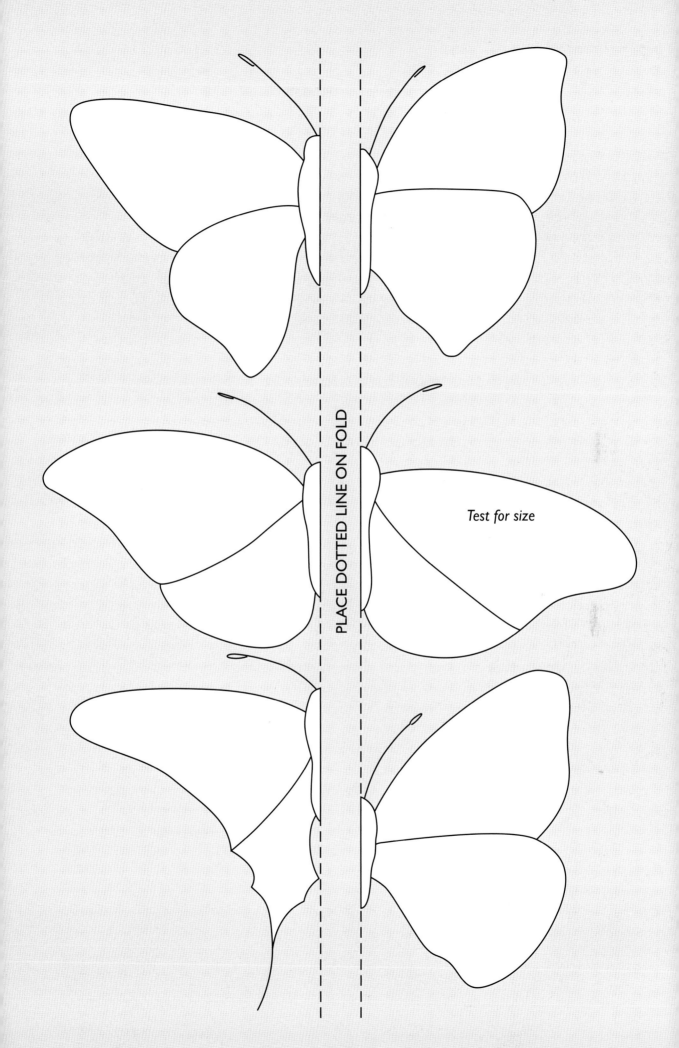

PLACE DOTTED LINE ON FOLD

Test for size

ALL A FLUTTER

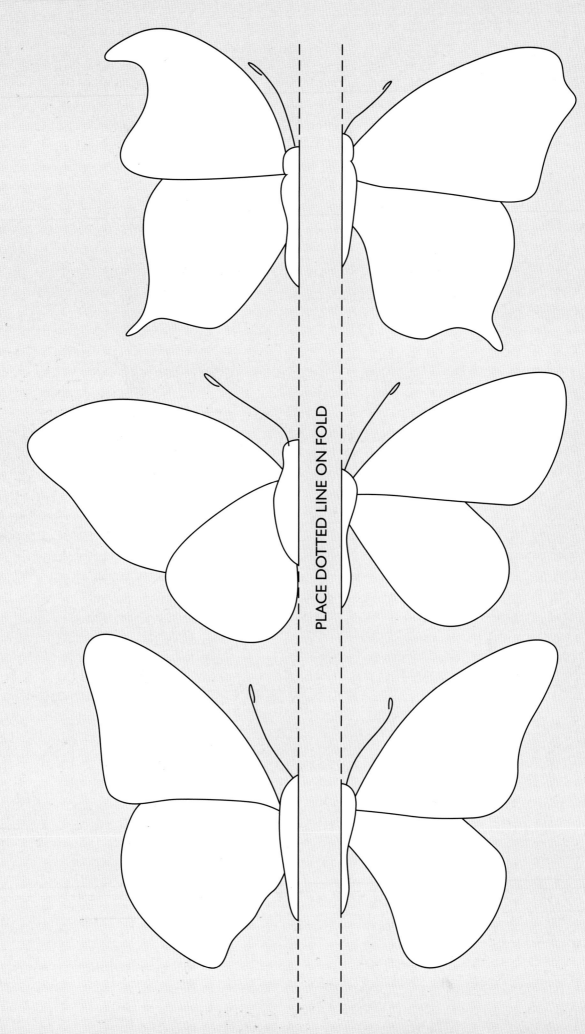

PLACE DOTTED LINE ON FOLD

EKUTHULENI – Pat Parker

Place of beauty and peace

37" x 24" (100cm x 70cm)

EKUTHULENI

This is a simple design most suitable for beginner quilters that is enhanced by the use of a few beads and decorative yarn.

Techniques

May be pieced and quilted either by hand or machine.

Materials

Background fabric	1 yd	(1m)
Black fabric	¼ yd	(30cm)
Blue fabric	¼ yd	(30cm)
Contrasting blue fabric	¼ yd	(30cm)
Brown fabric for rectangles and binding.	¾ yd	(80cm)
Batting	43" x 30"	(115cm x 85cm)
Backing	43" x 30"	(115cm x 85cm)
Decorative beads		
Decorative yarn		

Method

Make templates (1), (2), (3), (4) and (5) then add ¼" (10mm) seam allowance when cutting fabric.

Using blue fabric cut 8 x template (1), 1 x template (3), and 1 x template (5)

Using contrasting blue fabric cut 8 x template (2)

Using background fabric cut 2 x template (4).

Join triangles cut from (1) and (2) to form 4 rectangles. Set aside.

Now using background fabric cut:

8 × (A)	$4\frac{1}{2}$" × $1\frac{1}{2}$"	(120mm × 50mm)
8 × (B)	$3\frac{1}{2}$" × 2"	(100mm × 60mm)
8 × (C)	$7\frac{1}{2}$" × 2"	(200mm × 60mm)
8 × (D)	$5\frac{1}{2}$" × $2\frac{1}{2}$"	(160mm × 70mm)
8 × (E)	$11\frac{1}{2}$" × $2\frac{1}{2}$"	(300mm × 70mm)
8 × (F)	$8\frac{1}{2}$" × 3"	(240mm × 80mm)

Using brown fabric cut:

8 × (G)	2" × $1\frac{1}{2}$"	(60mm × 50mm)
8 × (H)	$2\frac{1}{2}$" × 2"	(70mm × 60mm)
8 × (J)	3" × $2\frac{1}{2}$"	(80mm × 70mm)

Using black fabric cut:

8 × (G)	2" × $1\frac{1}{2}$"	(60mm × 50mm)
8 × (H)	$2\frac{1}{2}$" × 2"	(70mm × 60mm)
8 × (J)	3" × $2\frac{1}{2}$"	(80mm × 70mm)

Piece 4 central blocks according to diagram.

Place your 4 blocks 2 across by 2 down as shown on layout diagram. Take 2 left blocks and join these with strip (F).

Now sew an (F) strip to top and bottom. Repeat for right side blocks.

Join (J) + (E) + (J) + (E) + (J) to form a long strip. Repeat twice.

Take one of these strips and sew to center of pieced blocks.

Now sew one to each side of work.

Using background fabric cut 2 pieces $22\frac{1}{2}$" × $2\frac{1}{2}$" (610mm × 60mm) (K). Sew to top and bottom of quilt.

Cut 2 pieces 34" × $2\frac{1}{2}$" (840mm × 60mm) (L). Sew to left and right sides of quilt.

Now quilt and bind top. Add decorative beads and/or yarn. (It is best to first quilt and then add beads otherwise the beads get caught up in your quilting threads.)

Now you can make triangle at base of quilt.

Piece triangle as shown.

Quilt, then bind 2 short sides of triangle. Sew triangle to back of quilt just above the binding.

Using blue fabric cut 4 squares 4" × 4" (100mm × 100mm).

Fold in half diagonally twice to make prairie points. Position 2 of these on each side of large triangle and sew to back of quilt.

Measure the exact width of quilt (including binding) and cut a strip of backing fabric that length x 1" (30mm). Turn in $\frac{1}{2}$" (10 mm) on all sides and cover raw edges on back of quilt.

Hand sew around all 4 sides with small hemming stitch.

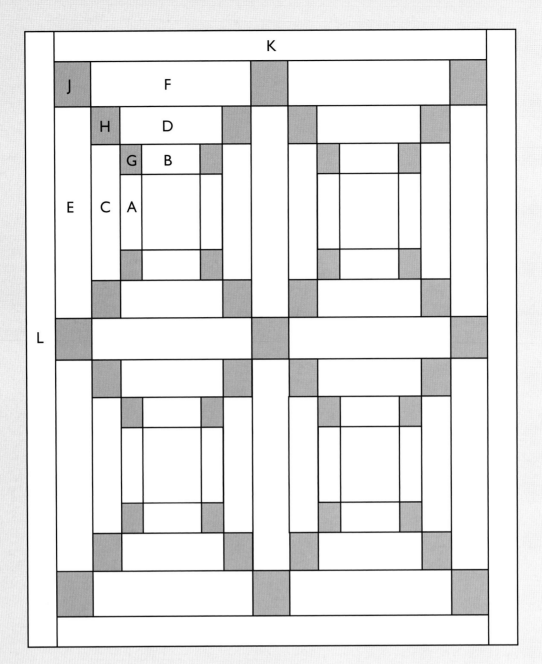

Quilt Layout

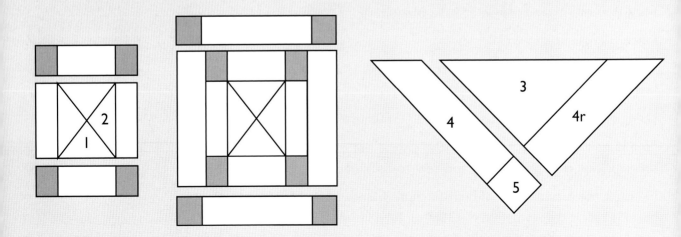

Piecing for 4 central blocks

Piecing for triangle

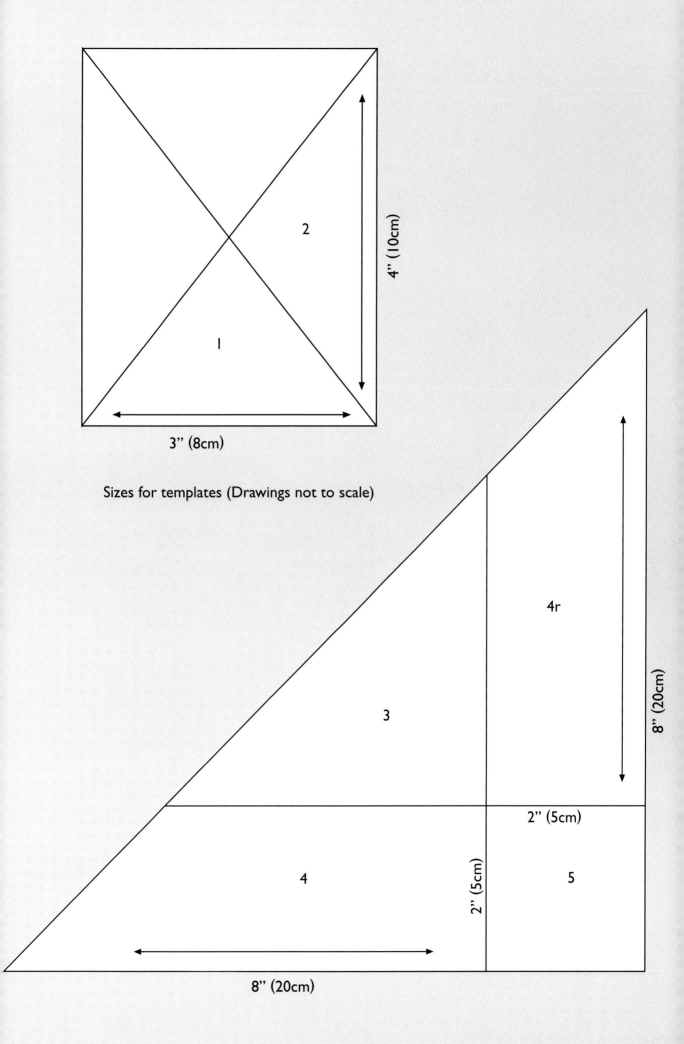

2

4" (10cm)

1

3" (8cm)

Sizes for templates (Drawings not to scale)

4r

8" (20cm)

3

2" (5cm)

4

2" (5cm)

5

8" (20cm)

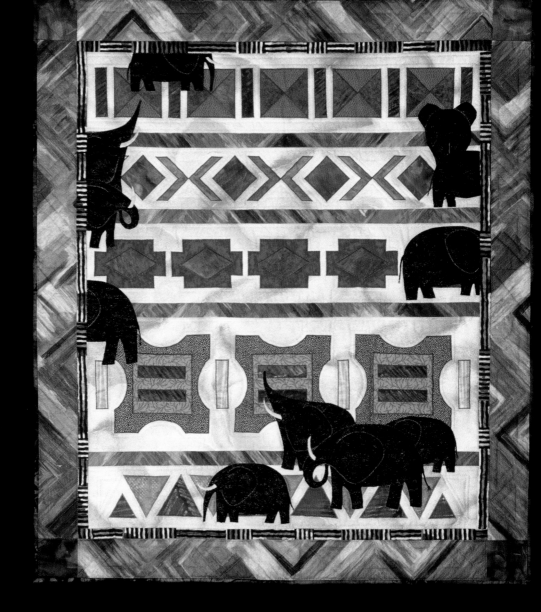

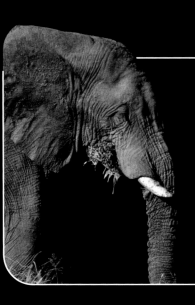

ELEPHANT HIDE – Pat Parker

41" x 46" (106cm x 120cm)

ELEPHANT HIDE

Elephants gather in family groups, but in spite of their size manage to 'hide' in the bush!

Techniques

May be appliquéd, pieced and quilted either by hand or machine.

Materials

Background fabric for strips	1 1/2 yd	(1.5m)
10 Fabrics suitable for motifs	1/4 yd each	(.25m each)
Fabric suitable for elephants	1/4 yd	(.25m)
Sashing strips and outer border	1 1/4 yd	(1.25m)
Inner border	1/2 yd	(.5m)
Backing	47" x 52"	(120cm x 135cm)
Batting	47" x 52"	(120cm x 135cm)
Binding	1/2 yd	(.5m)

Method

Please enlarge elephants. They should be doubled in size.

Using background fabric cut 5 strips the following sizes:

Strip 1	33 1/2" x 7"	(860mm x 180mm)
Strip 2	33 1/2" x 5 1/2"	(860mm x 140mm)
Strip 3	33 1/2" x 7"	(860mm x 180mm)
Strip 4	33 1/2" x 11"	(860mm x 290mm)
Strip 5	33 1/2" x 6"	(860mm x 160mm)

Referring to quilt photograph applique your geometric shapes onto the strips.

Cut 4 sashing strips 33$\frac{1}{2}$" x 1$\frac{1}{2}$" (860mm x 50mm)

Join 4 sashing strips to 5 background strips.

Using inner border fabric cut 2 strips 38$\frac{1}{2}$" x 1$\frac{1}{2}$" (990mm x 50mm) (A). Add to left and right hand sides of quilt.

Cut 2 strips 35$\frac{1}{2}$" x 1$\frac{1}{2}$" (920mm x 50mm) (B) and add to top and bottom of quilt.

Using outer border fabric cut 2 strips 40$\frac{1}{2}$" x 3$\frac{1}{2}$" (1050mm x 100mm) (C). Add to left and right hand sides of quilt.

Cut 2 strips 35$\frac{1}{2}$" x 3$\frac{1}{2}$" (920mm x 100mm) (D).

Using a contrast fabric cut 4 squares 3$\frac{1}{2}$" x 3$\frac{1}{2}$" (100mm x 100mm) (E).

Join a square to each end of (D). Sew to top and bottom of quilt.

Now appliqué elephants onto quilt top.

Quilt as desired and bind quilt.

E	D	
	B	
	Strip 1	
	Strip 2	
	Strip 3	
C A	Strip 4	
	Strip 5	

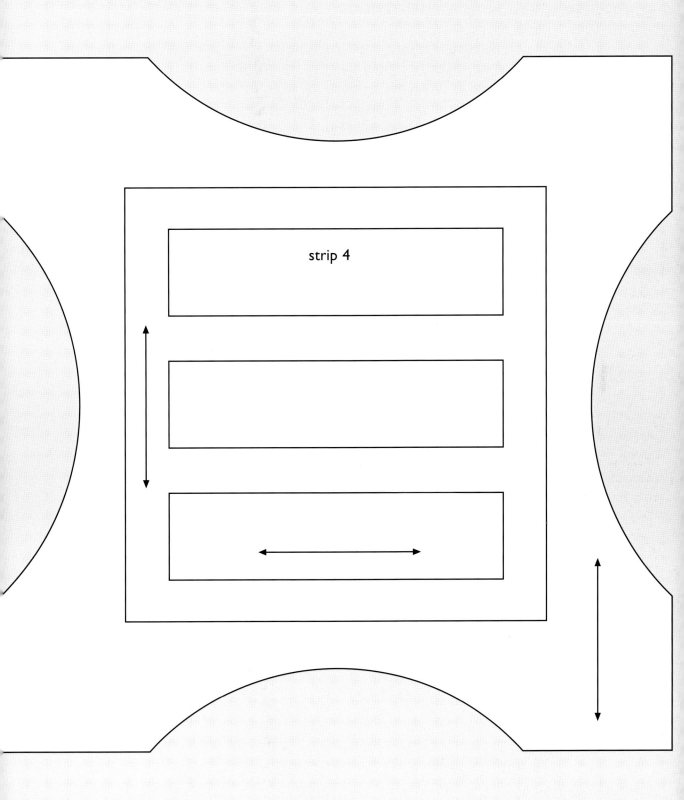

strip 4

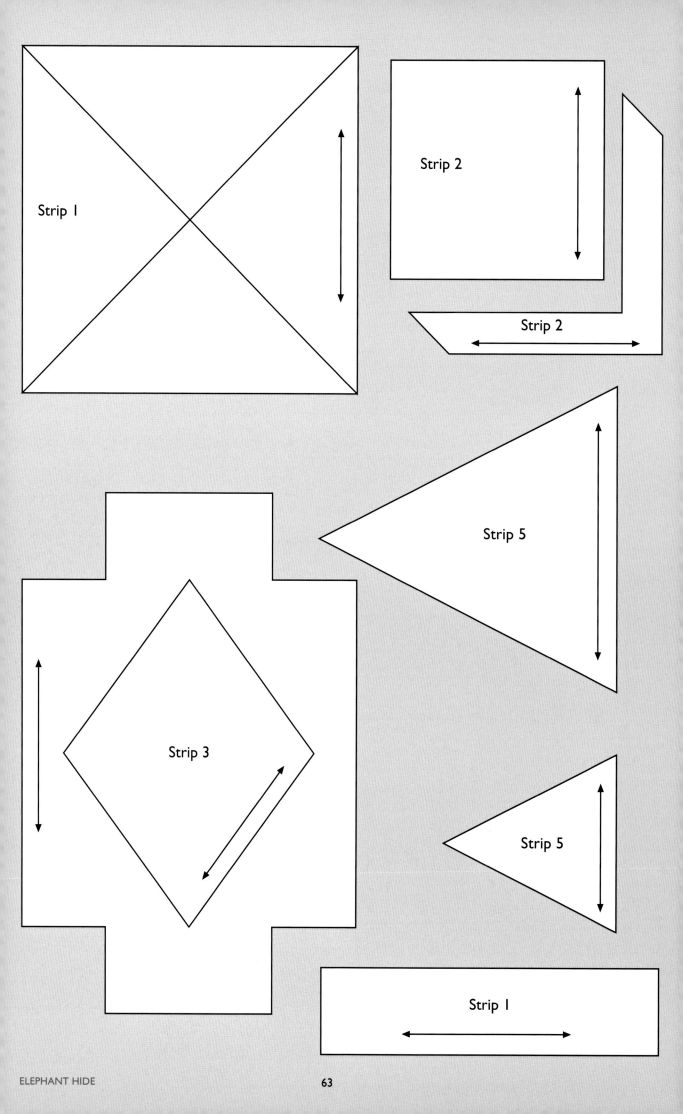

ELEPHANT HIDE

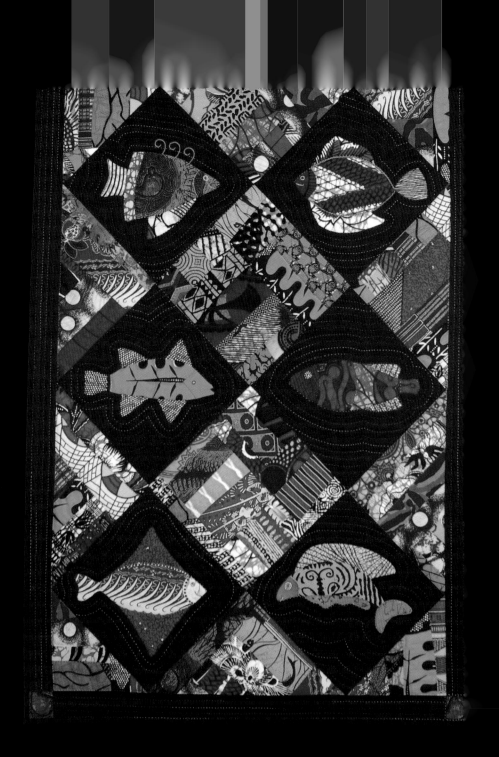

FANCIFUL FISH – Jenny Williamson and Pat Parker

25" x 37" (65cm x 94cm)

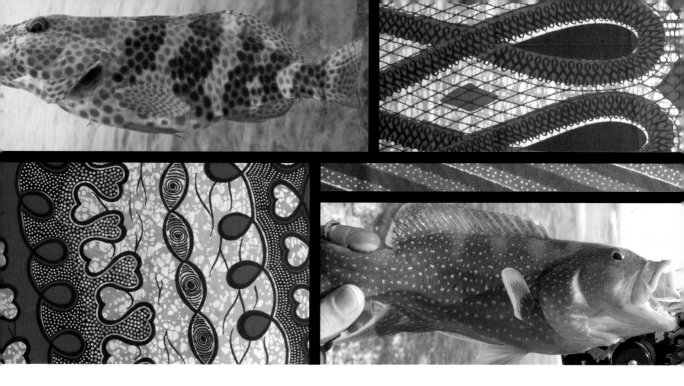

FANCIFUL FISH

Quicker to catch than quilt?!

Block Size

8" x 8" (20cm x 20cm) on point. You will need 8 blocks, 6 appliquéd and 2 pieced.

Techniques

May be appliquéd, embroidered and quilted by hand or machine. Piecing should be done by machine.

Materials

Background fabric for fish, final border

and binding.	1½ yd	(1.5m)
Batting	32" x 43"	(80 cm x 110cm)
Backing	32" x 43"	(80cm x 110cm)

Embroidery threads

Selection of at least 12 different fat quarters to be used for fishes and pieced blocks.

Method

N.B. The fish need to be enlarged.

Please cut an 8" x 8" (20cm x 20cm) square out of paper.

Take fish marked "test for size" and have this enlarged so that it fits diagonally well across your paper square. There should be a 1" (25mm) gap on all sides. This same percentage of enlargement should then be used for the remaining 5 fish.

Using background fabric cut 6 squares 8$\frac{1}{2}$" x 8$\frac{1}{2}$" (220mm x 220mm)(A). Appliqué fish to these 6 blocks.

Now make strips to be used for central blocks (B), border triangles (C) and corner triangles (D) as follows:

Cut one strip from your 12 different fabrics 18" x 5" (460mm x 130mm). Place these fabrics together in pairs – one above the other – with right sides facing upwards (you will have 6 pairs).

Using rotary cutter make a curved cut lengthwise on each pair. (Do not make curves too severe or the stitching will be difficult.)

Now take the top LEFT hand fabric and bottom RIGHT hand fabric. With right sides facing sew together. Press seam allowance to one side. Take bottom LEFT hand and top RIGHT hand fabric. With right sides facing sew together. Press seam allowance to one side. Repeat this procedure until all 6 pairs have been sewn. (You may need to repeat this procedure if you run short of strips).

Sew these strips together, making some of the strips horizontal and some vertical (see diagram) until they are approximately 10"(250mm) square.

It is a good idea to cut an 8"(200mm) square window out of cardboard and place this over your pieced fabrics. This will help you find the most pleasing configuration. Do this also with your triangles.

Your 2 central squares (B) should be cut 8$\frac{1}{2}$" x 8$\frac{1}{2}$" (220mm x 220mm). Your triangles (C) and (D) should be cut to the sizes specified on cutting diagrams.

Join pieces together in rows according to piecing diagram.

For the accurate length of your final border strips, measure across the centre of your pieced top horizontally. Using background fabric cut 2 strips this measured length x 2$\frac{1}{2}$" (70mm) (E). Sew to top and bottom of quilt.

Now measure across your pieced top vertically and cut 2 strips this measured length x 2$\frac{1}{2}$" (70mm)(F).

Cut 4 corner squares from a contrasting fabric 2$\frac{1}{2}$" x 2$\frac{1}{2}$" (70mm x 70mm)(G)

Sew a square to each end of your 2 strips then join to left and right hand sides of quilt.

Quilt as desired.

Bind quilt with background fabric.

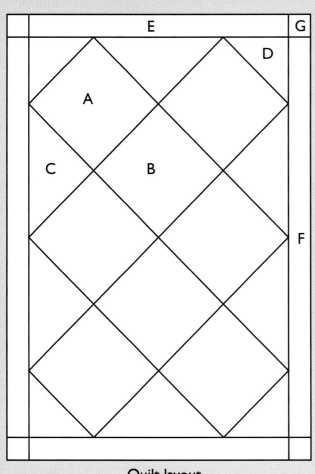

Quilt layout

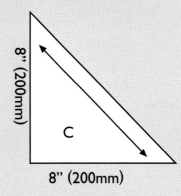

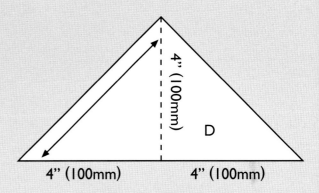

Piecing diagram

Piecing guide for B

FANCIFUL FISH

Test for size

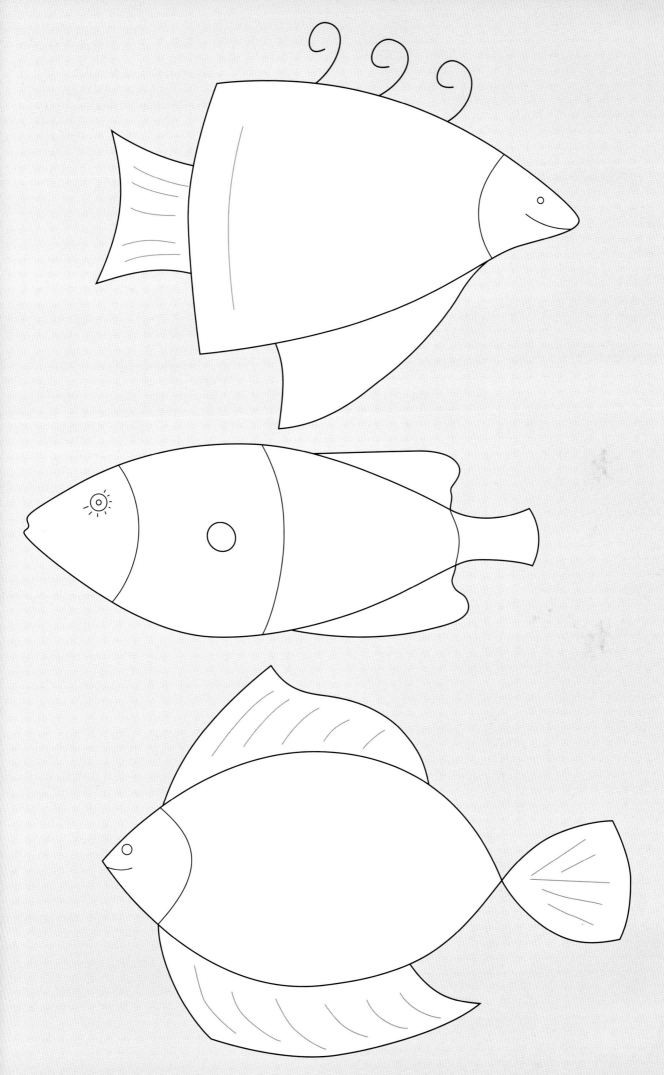

LADUMA – Jenny Williamson and Pat Parker

40" x 42" (102cm x 108cm)

LADUMA

Laduma means Goal! This quilt could just as easily be called Practice Makes Perfect – just as applicable to quilting as it is to soccer!

Techniques

Hand appliquéd, embroidered and quilted – machine pieced.

Materials

Background fabric   1 yd   (1m)

A selection of different printed fabrics for all appliqué and border.*

*You will need 18 pieces of fabric 18" x 5"(460mm x 130mm) to make up your border strips. These need not all be different, but the larger your selection the better the end result. In other words you can repeat some of the fabrics if necessary.

Backing   46" x 48"   (117cm x 123cm)

Batting   46" x 48"   (117cm x 123cm)

Binding   ½ yd   (.5m)

Method

N.B. The appliqué shapes need to be enlarged. Take shop marked "test for size" and have this enlarged so that it measures 6" (15cm) across. This same percentage of enlargement should then be used for all the appliqué shapes.

Cut background fabric 31½" x 33½" (800mm x 860mm)

Using photograph as guide do all applique and embroidery.

Cut 18 pieces of fabric 18" x 5" (460mm x 130mm). Place these fabrics together in pairs – one above the other – with right sides facing upwards (you will have 9 pairs).

Using rotary cutter make a curved cut lengthwise on each pair.

(Do not make curves too severe or the stitching will be difficult.)

Now take the top LEFT hand fabric and bottom RIGHT hand fabric. With right sides facing sew together. Press seam allowance to one side. Take bottom LEFT hand and top RIGHT hand fabric. With right sides facing sew together. Press seam allowance to one side. Repeat this procedure until all 9 pairs have been sewn.

Join these strips together lengthwise in order to use them for your border.

Cut 2 pieces 31^{1}/2" x 5" (800mm x 130mm) Sew these to top and bottom of quilt.

Cut 2 pieces 42^{1}/2" x 5" (1080mm x 130mm) Sew these to left and right hand sides of quilt.

Shadow quilt in rows approximately ^{1}/2" (6mm) apart. Bind quilt.

Test for size

SHOP

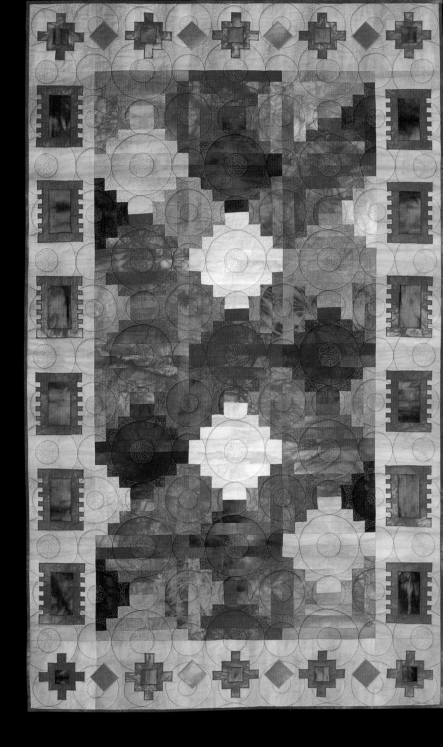

NOT QUITE THE COURT HOUSE STEPS –

Jenny Williamson and Pat Parker

Quilted by: Petro van Rooyen

37" x 61" (92cm x 152cm)

NOT QUITE THE COURT HOUSE STEPS

Many geometric patterns have been used for centuries by African women to decorate the walls and window surrounds of their homes. In many instances the similarity to traditional quilting designs is remarkable.

Techniques

Machine appliquéd, pieced and quilted.

Block Size

8" x 8" (20cm x 20cm). You will need 18 blocks, 3 across by 6 down.

Materials

A selection of quilters quarters (at least 12) – hand-dyes are good.

Fabric for border	1 yd	(1m)
Batting	43" x 67"	(107cm x 167cm)
Backing	43" x 67"	(107cm x 167cm)
Binding	½ yd	(.5m)

Method

Make templates according to the sizes given on diagram and add seam allowances to these sizes.

You will use the same template for Nos. 1, 2, 3 and 4. Same template for Nos. 5, 6, 7 and 8, same template for Nos. 9, 10, 11 and 12 and same template for Nos. 13 and 14.

Using colour photograph as guide, piece each block in numerical order as per diagram using 4 different fabrics for each block. (A) will be one fabric, (B) another, (C) another and (D) another.

Make 18 blocks (3 x 6).

Join blocks in rows.

For the accurate length of your border strips, measure across the centre of your pieced top horizontally. Using border fabric cut 2 strips this measured length x 6½" (170mm).

Now measure across your pieced top vertically and cut 2 strips this measured length x 6½" (170mm).

Cut 4 corner squares 6½" x 6½" (170mm x 170mm).

Applique borders and corner squares omitting the squares on point at top and bottom corners. (These should be appliquéd after border has been sewn in place).

Sew the 2 horizontal borders to top and bottom of quilt.

Sew a square to each end of your 2 vertical borders then join to left and right hand sides of quilt.

Now appliqué squares on point at top and bottom corners.

Quilt as desired and bind.

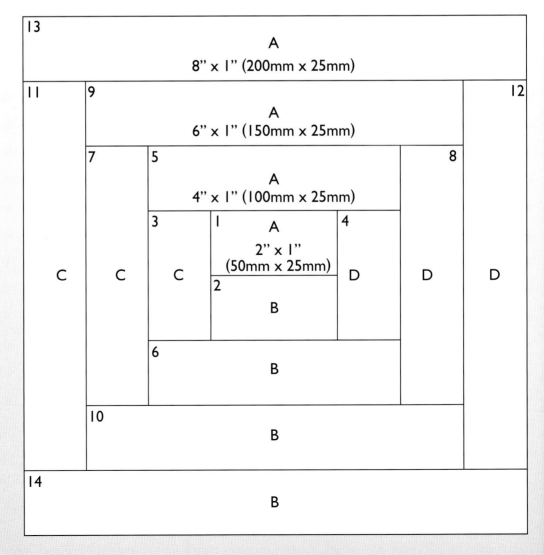

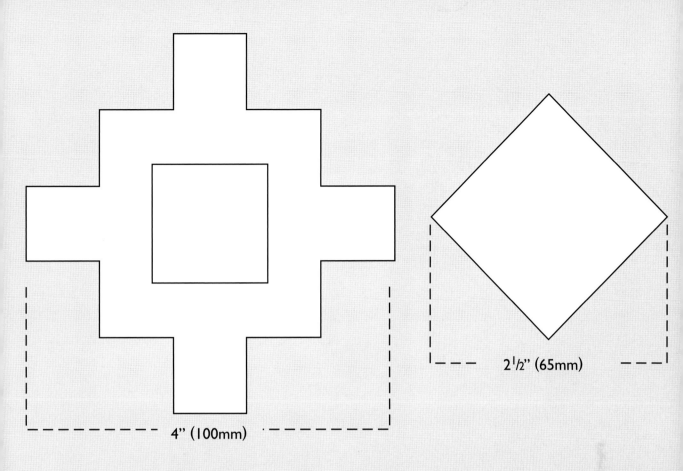

4" (100mm)

2½" (65mm)

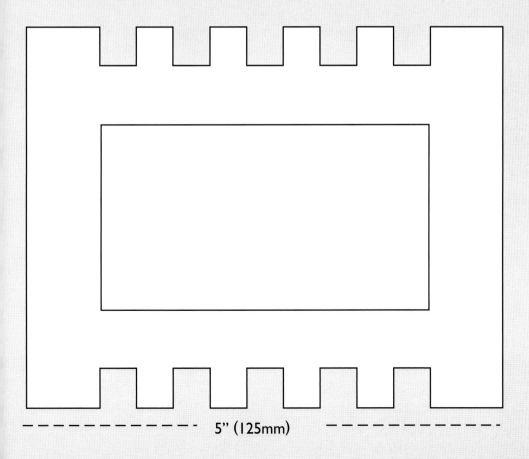

5" (125mm)

NOT QUITE THE COURT HOUSE STEPS

ROAD TO UMTATA – Jenny Williamson and Pat Parker

52" x 38" (132cm x 96cm)

ROAD TO UMTATA

Techniques

The appliqué, piecing and quilting may be done either by hand or machine.

Block Size

12" x 12" (300mm x 300mm). Make 6 blocks.

Materials

Background fabric	1 yd	(1m)
Sashing strips	1 yd	(1m)
Sashing squares	1/4 yd	(25cm)
Inner border	1/2 yd	(50cm)
Outer border	1 1/2 yd	(1.5 m)
Backing	58" x 44"	(147cm x 110cm)
Batting	58" x 44"	(147cm x 110cm)

Small scraps of brightly colored fabrics suitable for appliqué.

Method

Cut 6 background squares 12 1/2" x 12 1/2" (320mm x 320mm) (A).

Then using the quilt photograph for reference appliqué 6 squares.

Cut 17 sashing strips 12 1/2" x 2 1/2" (320mm x70mm) (B) and 12 sashing squares 2 1/2" x 2 1/2" (70mm x 70mm) (C).

Lay out the blocks 3 across by 2 down.

Working with the top 3 blocks join from left to right sewing a sashing strip (B) to the left side of each block and another strip to the right hand edge. Do the same with the second set of 3 blocks.

Sew 4 sashing squares (C) to 3 sashing strips (B) alternating the squares and strips to form a row.

Make another 2 of these rows, then sew these 5 rows together.

Using border fabrics

Cut 2 strips 30$\frac{1}{2}$" x 1$\frac{1}{2}$" (770mm x 50mm)(D)

Cut 2 strips 44$\frac{1}{2}$" x 1$\frac{1}{2}$" (1120mm x 50mm)(E)

Cut 4 squares 1$\frac{1}{2}$" x 1$\frac{1}{2}$" (50mm x 50mm)(F)

Cut 2 strips 32$\frac{1}{2}$" x 3$\frac{1}{2}$" (830mm x 100mm)(G)

Cut 2 strips 46$\frac{1}{2}$" x 3$\frac{1}{2}$" (1180mm x 100mm)(H)

Cut 4 squares 3$\frac{1}{2}$" x 3$\frac{1}{2}$" (100mm x 100mm)(J)

Sew strips (D) to left and right hand sides of quilt.

Join 2 squares (F) to either end of strips (E). Sew to top and bottom of quilt.

Sew strips (G) to left and right hand sides of quilt.

Join 2 squares (J) to either end of strips (H). Sew to top and bottom of quilt.

Embellish your quilt with some embroidery. Shadow quilt in rows on backgrounds approximately $\frac{1}{4}$" (6mm) apart.

Bind quilt.

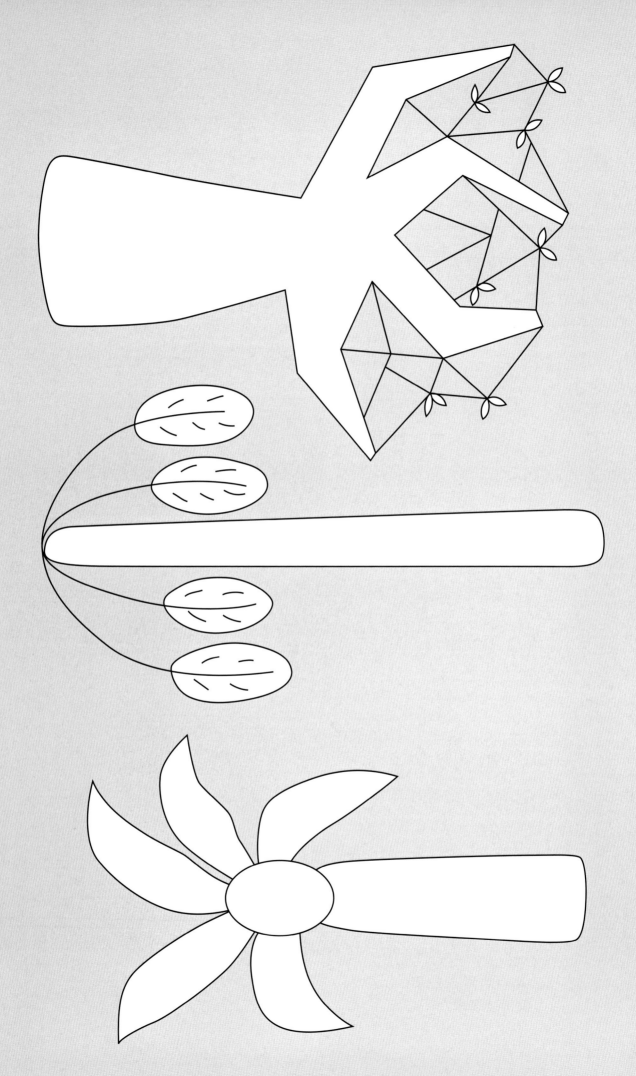

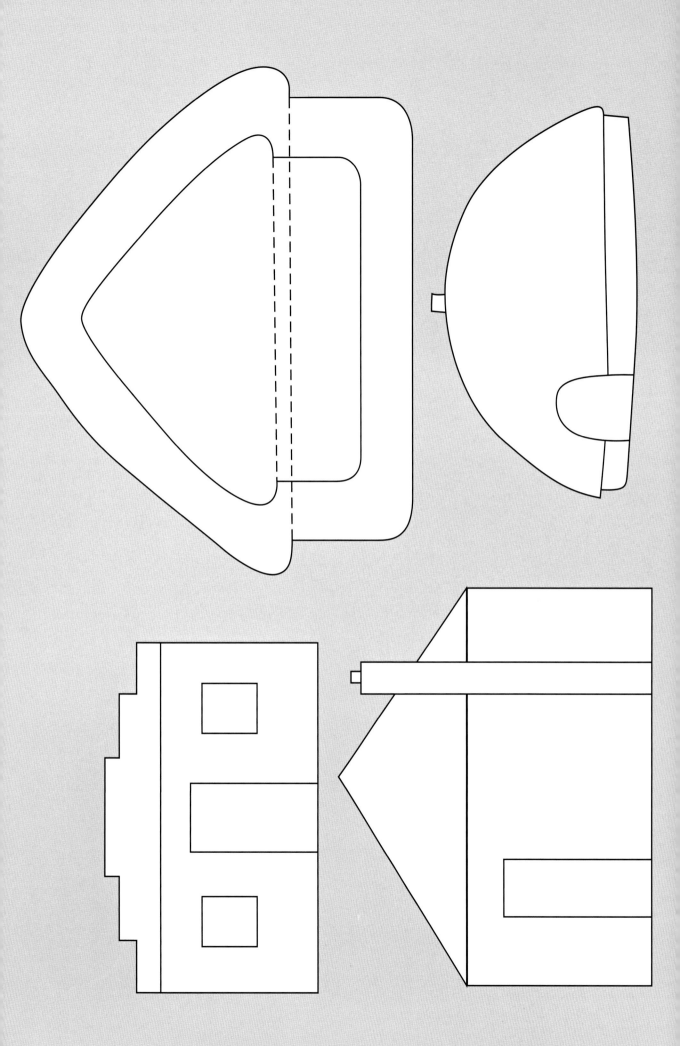

SCATTERINGS OF AFRICA – Jenny Williamson

36" x 46" (91cm x 117 cm)

SCATTERINGS OF AFRICA

The inspiration for this quilt was found in the African murals that are drawn by the artists freehand, therefore they are never accurately measured. This gives a naïve character to their art, which is the look I wished to convey in this quilt. We have provided some appliqué shapes, but we suggest you choose a few of your own. Choose whatever shapes you find personify 'Africa', e.g. a particular tree, flower, animal, bird, etc. You would then appliqué the shapes you have chosen in rows across the background strips.

This quilt can be made any size. We suggest, however, that the width is not more than 43" (110cm), as it is more economical if the background and sashing strips are cut across the width of the fabric. Once you have decided upon the width of the quilt make as many background strips as are required to give the desired length.

Techniques

Machine appliquéd, pieced and quilted. Applique and quilting can be done by hand if preferred.

Materials

The larger the variety of fabrics the better the quilt will look. Therefore you will need a variety of the following:

Pieces suitable for backgrounds	1/4 yd	(25cm)
Pieces suitable for the sashing strips and the appliqué.	1/4 yd	(25cm)

N.B. These must not be quilters' quarters — they must be the full width of the fabrics.

Batting and backing 6"(15cm) larger both horizontally and vertically than the quilt top.

Binding	½ yd	(50cm)
Iron-on vylene	1 yd	(1m)

Appliqué and embroidery threads.

Method

Cut your background strips in the following manner.

Decide upon the horizontal measurement of your quilt (less the outside border). Cut your background strips this measurement by whatever depths are necessary for the shapes that you intend to appliqué.

Appliqué the shapes you have chosen to the background strips.

Cut sashing strips the same measurement across as the background strips, but vary the vertical measurements.

Intersperse your sashing and background strips. Move them around until you are satisfied with the result.

Join all strips. (You may wish to insert a few narrow pleats and prairie points here and there to add interest).

Embellish the quilt with either machine or hand embroidery.

Frame your quilt with suitable fabric choosing a second fabric for the corner blocks.

Quilt around the appliqué shapes and along some of the sashing strips to keep the work from stretching.

Bind quilt.

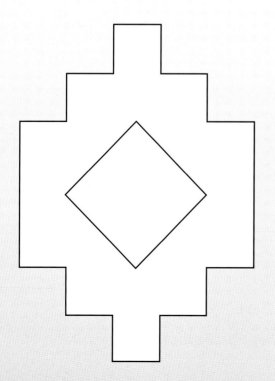
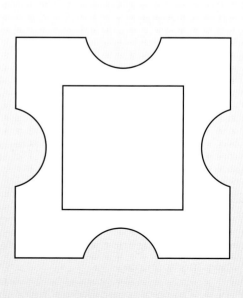

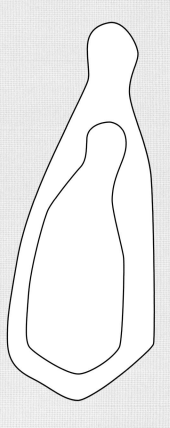

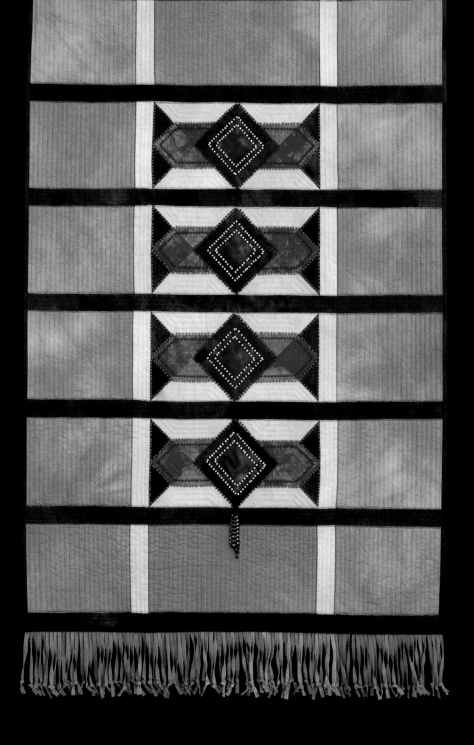

SERENITY – Pat Parker

32" x 48" (80cm x 120cm)

SERENITY

This is a simple design. I feel, therefore, that some embellishment is necessary. This can be done with either embroidery or, as is the case here, with a single line of beading.

Techniques

This quilt may be hand or machine pieced and quilted.

Materials

Main color (background)	I yd	(1m)
Cream	$^1/_2$ yd	(50cm)
Black (includes binding)	I yd	(1m)
Tan	$^1/_2$ yd	(50cm)
Blue	$^1/_4$ yd	(25 cm)
Batting	38" x 54"	(95cm x 135cm)
Backing	38" x 54"	(95cm x 135cm)

Method

Using layout diagram as guide cut the following:

Background fabric (No. 1 on diagram) Cut 12 – 6$^1/_2$" x 8$^1/_2$" (170mm x 220mm)

Background fabric (No. 2 on diagram) Cut 2 – 6$^1/_2$" x 12$^1/_2$" (170mm x 320mm)

Cream fabric (No. 3 on diagram) Cut 12 – 6$^1/_2$" x 2" (170mm x 60mm)

Black fabric (No. 4 on diagram) Cut 7 – 31$^1/_2$" x 2" (800mm x 60mm)

To make accurate templates, take a sheet of paper and draw a rectangle 6" x 12" (150mm x 300mm) and mark according to template diagram.

You can then cut your templates according to your sizes on your sheet of paper. This is easy to do and your templates will be 100% accurate.

Now using templates cut fabric for the 4 pieced sections of the central panel.

A – Cut 4   B – Cut 8   C – Cut 8   D – Cut 16

E – Cut 16   F – Cut 8   G – Cut 16

Using piecing diagrams as guide piece these 4 sections. The numbers on piecing diagrams give the order in which the pieces should be joined.

Now join quilt as follows: Rows 1 to 6 = 1 + 3 + 2 + 3 + 1.

Add black sashing strips, one between each panel and one at each end.

You are now ready to quilt and bind.

Add fringe last as follows: Cut approximately 120 pieces of background fabric 6" x 1" (150mm x 25mm). Fold in long edges $^1/_4$" (6mm) and then fold again so that you have a piece $^1/_4$" (6mm) wide with no raw edges showing. Sew one row of machine stitching along length to hold in place. Tie knot at one end. Baste these strands along back of quilt so that there are no gaps between strands of fringe. Now using a strip of black fabric make an additional binding on back of quilt to cover raw edges and hold fringe in place.

Layout diagram

Template diagram

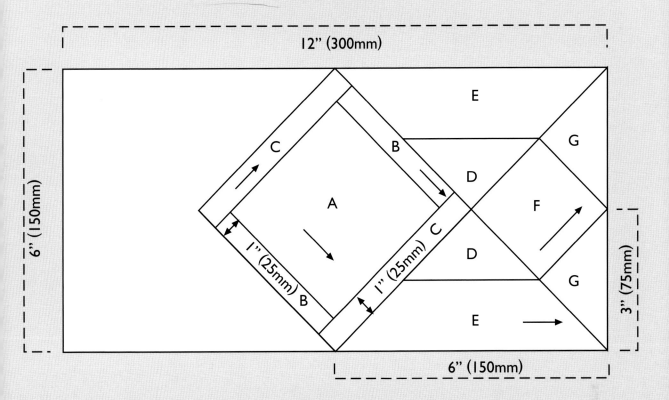

12" (300mm)

6" (150mm)

E

C

B

D

G

A

F

C

D

1" (25mm) B

1" (25mm) C

D

G

B

E

3" (75mm)

6" (150mm)

Piecing diagram

8

4

2

9

11

1

10

3

5

6

12

7

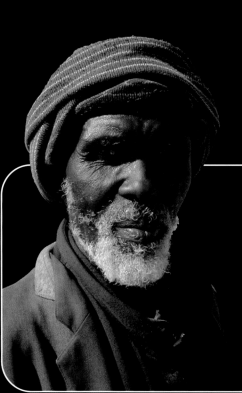

SIMUNYE VILLAGE – Jenny Williamson and Pat Parker

36" x 41" (93cm x 107cm)

SIMUNYE VILLAGE

Simunye meaning "We are One'.

Techniques

Can be appliquéd, pieced and quilted either by hand or machine.

Materials

Background fabric (not too busy)	I yd	(Im)

A variety of brightly colored fabrics suitable for all the appliqué and also for borders.

Batting	42" x 47"	(105cm x 120cm)
Backing	42" x 47"	(105cm x 120 cm)
Binding	$^{1}/_{2}$ yd	(50cm)
Iron-on vylene	I yd	(Im)

Appliqué and embroidery threads.

Method

Cut I piece of background fabric 20$^{1}/_{2}$" x 28$^{1}/_{2}$" (520mm x 720mm) (A).

Cut 3 pieces of background fabric 8$^{1}/_{2}$" x 10$^{1}/_{2}$" (220mm x 270mm) (B) (C) and (D). Using the photograph of quilt as guide appliqué these 4 pieces of fabric.

Cut border strip 28$^{1}/_{2}$" x 2$^{1}/_{2}$" (720mm x 70mm) (E). This may be one fabric or may be divided into blocks using a number of fabrics.

Sew to right hand side of (A).

Cut (H) 22$^{1}/_{2}$" x 6$^{1}/_{2}$" (570mm x 170mm). This may also be one fabric or may be divided into blocks using a number of fabrics.

Add (H) to (A) and (E).

Cut 2 different fabrics $8\frac{1}{2}$" x $2\frac{1}{2}$" (220mm x 70mm) for (F) and (G). Join (B) (F) (C) (G) and (D) to (A) and (H).

Cut top border (J) $30\frac{1}{2}$" x $3\frac{1}{2}$" (770mm x 100mm).

Join to top of quilt.

Cut (K) $37\frac{1}{2}$" x $3\frac{1}{2}$" (950mm x 100mm) and join to left hand side of quilt.

Cut (L) $33\frac{1}{2}$" x $4\frac{1}{2}$" (800mm x 120mm) and join to base of quilt.

Cut (M) $41\frac{1}{2}$" x $3\frac{1}{2}$" (1050mm x 100mm) and join to right hand side of quilt.

Embellish the quilt top with embroidery.

Shadow quilt in rows on background approximately $\frac{1}{4}$" (6mm) apart.

Bind quilt.

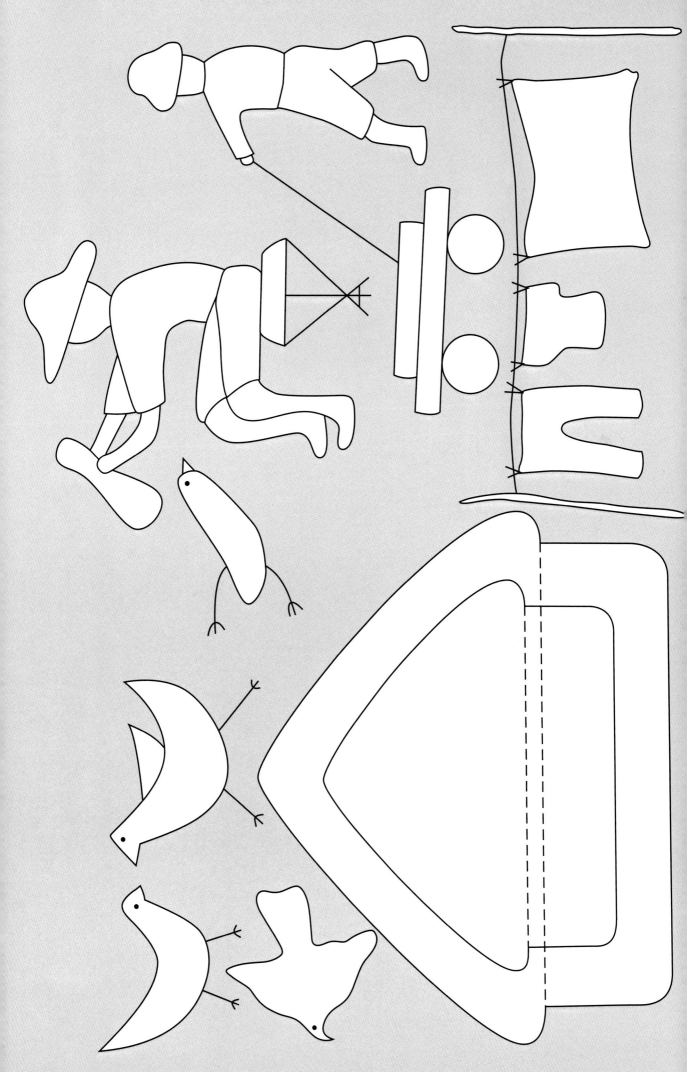

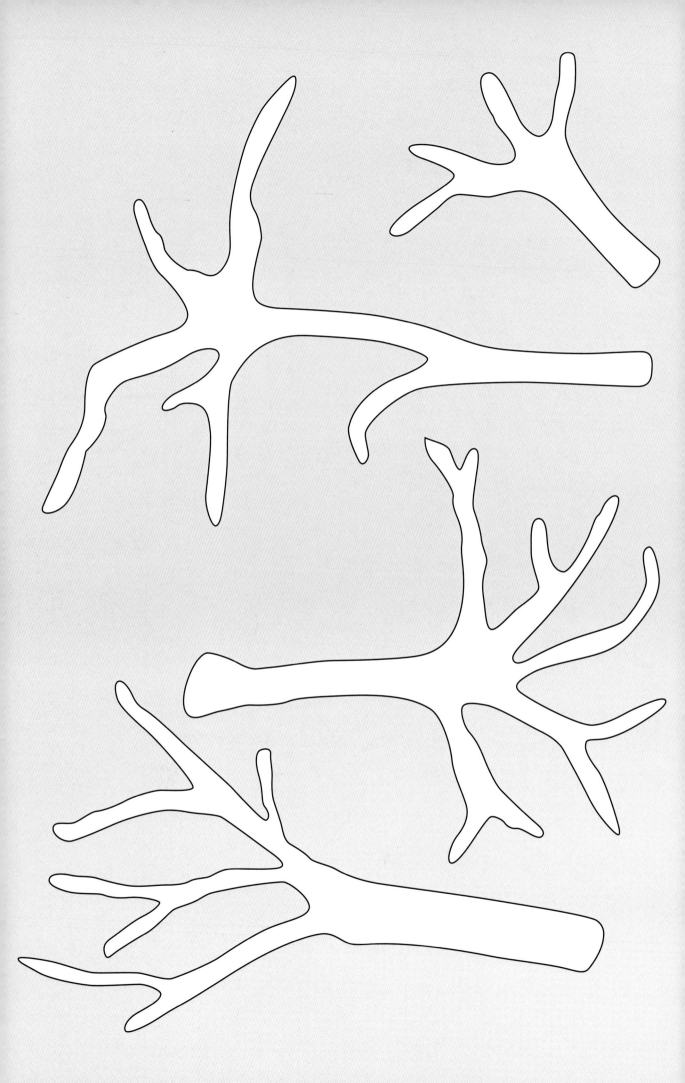

SUMMER MADNESS – Pat Parker

42" x 50" (108cm x 128cm)

SUMMER MADNESS

I chose to use the same fabrics for my flowers and leaves, but this design would work well if a selection of different fabrics was used, in other words this would work well as a 'scrap quilt'.

Techniques

May be appliquéd, pieced and quilted either by hand or machine.

Materials

Background fabric	1 ½ yd	(1.5m)
Main border fabric	1 ½ yd	(1.5m)
Flower fabric	½ yd	(.5m)
Stems and leaves	½ yd	(.5m)
Geometric shapes on appliqué border	½ yd	(.5m)
Fabric for dragonfly wings	¼ yd	(.25m)

A selection of fabrics for borders – scraps will do.

Backing	48" x 56"	(123cm x 143cm)
Batting	48" x 56"	(123cm x 142cm)
Binding	½ yd	(.5m)

Embroidery threads

Method

N.B. Please take the appliqué shape marked "test for size" and have this enlarged so that it measures 7½" (19cm) across.

This same percentage of enlargement should then be used for all the appliqué shapes.

Using background fabric cut the following sizes:

Centre piece 20$\frac{1}{2}$" x 28$\frac{1}{2}$" (520mm x 720mm) (A).

2 Strips 26$\frac{1}{2}$" x 5$\frac{1}{2}$" (680mm x 150mm) (B)

2 Strips 34$\frac{1}{2}$" x 5$\frac{1}{2}$" (880mm x 150mm) (C)

4 Squares 5$\frac{1}{2}$" x 5$\frac{1}{2}$"(150mm x 150mm) (D)

Using color photograph as guide do all appliqué except for corner flowers and leaves on border. These can only be done after quilt has been pieced.

Using main border fabric cut 8 squares 3$\frac{1}{2}$" x 3$\frac{1}{2}$" (100mm x 100mm) (G).

If hand piecing follow instructions from here to end.

If machine piecing over papers follow instructions for borders marked with *.

Using templates 1, 2 and 2r piece borders (E) and (F). (E) will have 10 triangles using a selection of fabrics and 9 triangles using main border fabric (all template 1), plus one template 2 and one template 2r at ends. (F) will have 14 triangles using a selection of fabrics and 13 using main border fabric, plus one template 2 and one template 2r at ends.

Now join pieced strips (E) to top and bottom of quilt.

Join squares (G) to either end of strips (F) and sew to left and right sides of quilt.

Now sew appliqué borders to top and bottom of quilt (B).

Sew squares (D) to each end of (C) and sew to left and right sides of quilt.

The corner flowers and leaves can now be appliquéd.

Piece borders (H) and (J) in the same manner as strips (E) and (F).

Sew strips (H) to top and bottom of quilt.

Add remaining squares (G) to strips (J) and sew to left and right sides of quilt.

Shadow quilt in rows $\frac{1}{4}$" (6mm) apart.

Bind quilt.

---

* machine piecing over papers instructions:

See template diagram for paper piecing. This gives you sizes for border (E).

Using same format draw templates for (F) (H) and (J).

The sizes are:

(F)	28$\frac{1}{2}$" x 3$\frac{1}{2}$"	(720mm x 100mm)
(H)	36$\frac{1}{2}$" x 3$\frac{1}{2}$"	(940mm x 100mm)
(J)	44$\frac{1}{2}$" x 3$\frac{1}{2}$"	(1140mm x 100mm)

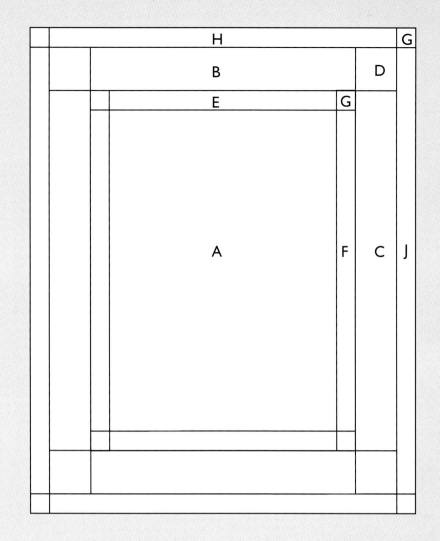

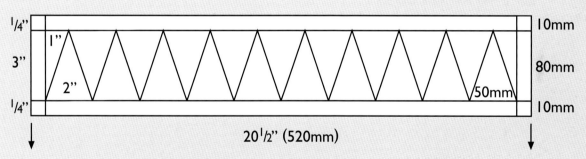

1/4"		10mm
3"		80mm
1/4"		10mm

1"

2"

50mm

20¹/₂" (520mm)

Template diagram for paper piecing (E)

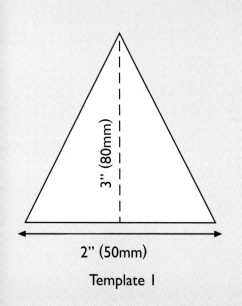

3" (80mm)

2" (50mm)

Template 1

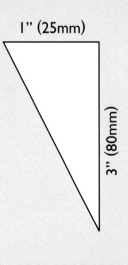

1" (25mm)

3" (80mm)

Template 2 and 2r

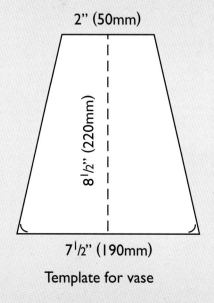

2" (50mm)

8¹/₂" (220mm)

7¹/₂" (190mm)

Template for vase

Test for size

Corner

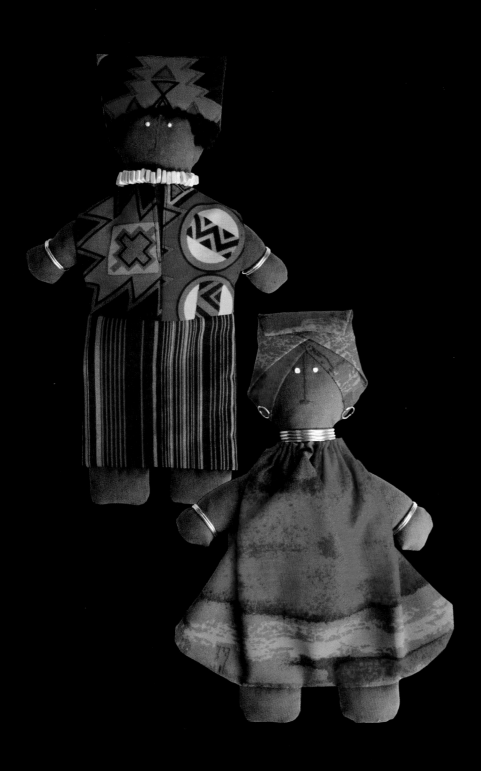

AFRICAN DOLLS – Jenny Williamson and Pat Parker

8" (20cm)

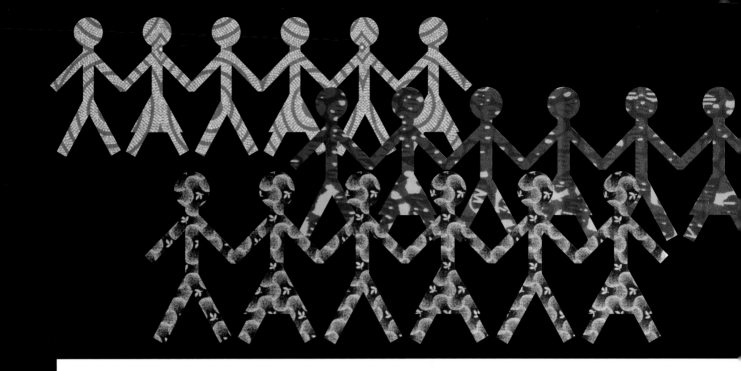

AFRICAN DOLLS

Her Name is THANDI (pronounced TANDY) meaning BELOVED.
His Name is SIPHO (pronounced SEEFO) meaning GIFT.

Techniques

Can be sewn either by hand or machine. If sewing by hand use a small backstitch.

INSTRUCTIONS FOR THANDI

Materials

Brown cotton fabric suitable for body and feet.	14" x 7" (360mm x 180mm)
Brightly colored fabric suitable for dress and headdress.	1/4 yd (25cm)

Small packet stuffing.

2 Split key rings 1" (25mm) in diameter (inside measurement)

2 Split key rings 5/8" (15mm) in diameter (inside measurement)

2 Small rings suitable for earrings.

1 x 20" (50cm) length strong black thread.

1 x 20" (50cm) length red embroidery thread.

1 x 20" (50cm) length white embroidery thread.

Method

Dress – cut 2

Body – cut 2

Feet – cut 4

Headdress – cut 1

$1/4$" (6mm) seam allowance used throughout.

Transfer all markings to fabric before sewing.

Body: Sew body leaving open at base. Clip corners, turn right side out. Stuff head firmly, place 2 large split key rings in position around neck. Stuff arms and body firmly and stitch base closed.

Feet: Sew feet leaving top open. Trim seams, turn right side out, stuff lightly and stitch top closed.

Dress: Turn under top of dress on foldline as indicated on pattern and press. With right sides facing sew the sides and base leaving open gaps for arms and feet.

Turn dress right side out and press lightly along the seams. Push feet through open gaps. Using small blind hemming stitches, stitch feet in position.

Starting at centre back and using strong black thread run a gathering stitch $1/4$" (6mm) from the top edge of dress ending where you started. Slip body into dress extending arms through side openings. Pull up gathering around neck and tie knot. Trim ends of thread.

Headdress: Turn in $1/4$" (6mm) on straight edge of headdress and press. Fold around head as indicated on diagrams. Stitch top of headdress down as indicated on diagram. Stitch headdress to head along edge of headdress, sewing earrings in position as you go.

Using 2 strands of embroidery thread embroider nose and eyes.

Use stem-stitch for nose and French-knots for eyes.

Place bracelets on arms.

INSTRUCTIONS FOR SIPHO

Materials

Brown cotton fabric suitable for body and feet	14" x 7"	(360mm x 180mm)
Brightly colored fabric suitable for shirt, trousers and hat.	$1/4$ yd	(25 cm)

Small packet stuffing.

2 Split key rings 5/8" (15mm) in diameter (inside measurement).

1 x 20" (50cm) length red embroidery thread.

1 x 20" (50cm) length white embroidery thread.

Beads suitable for necklace.

Black embroidery thread for hair.

Method

Body – cut 2

Feet – cut 4

Trousers – cut 2

Hat – cut 1

Shirt – cut 1 front and 1 back

¹/₄" (6mm) seam allowance used throughout.

Transfer all markings to fabric before sewing.

Sew body and feet exactly as instructions for Thandi leaving out split key rings around neck.

Sew centre front seam of shirt below mark. Iron open and topstitch around opening close to edge above mark.

Sew shoulder seams between marks.

Sew top of trousers to base of shirt.

Sew side seams as far as mark.

Fold in raw edges of neck and armholes and catch down by hand.

Turn in raw edge at base of trousers and topstitch close to edge.

Place feet between marks and using small blind hemming stitches, sew feet in place on front and back.

Now topstitch down centre of trousers below mark.

Fold hat on fold line (right sides facing) and stitch sides.

Trim corners and turn right side out.

Turn in raw edge and topstitch.

Using blind hemming stitches sew hat to head, slightly higher in front and lower at back. Add French-knots in black thread for hair.

Using 2 strands of embroidery thread embroider nose and eyes.

Use stem stitch for nose and French-knots for eyes.

Thread beads and tie tightly around neck.

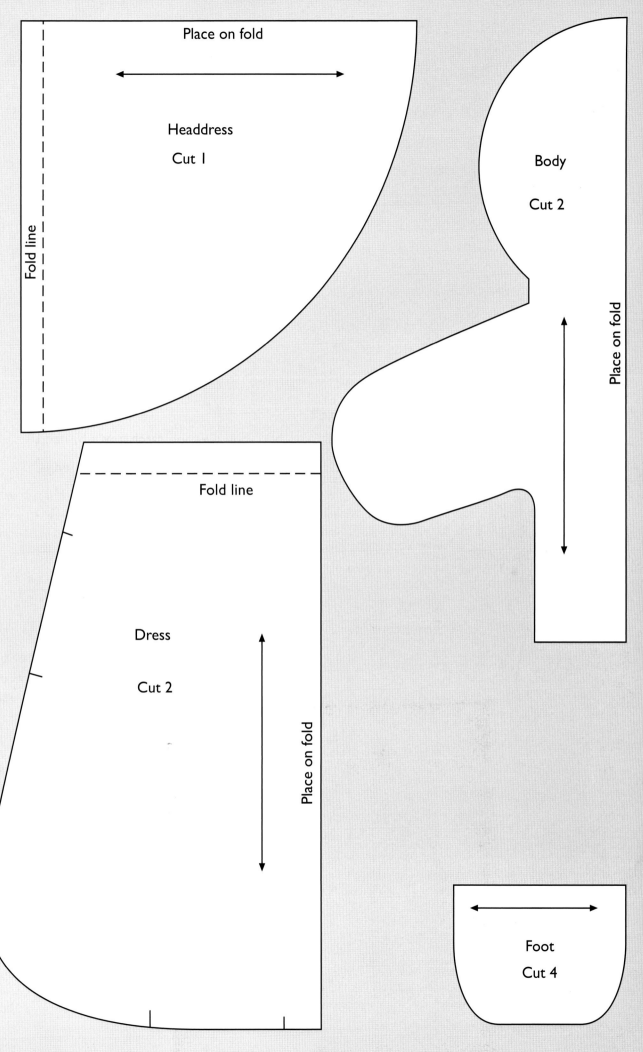

Place on fold

Headdress

Cut 1

Fold line

Body

Cut 2

Place on fold

Fold line

Dress

Cut 2

Place on fold

Foot

Cut 4

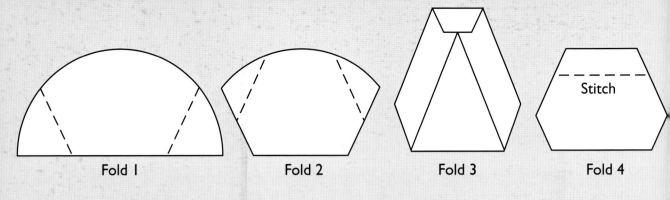

Fold 1   Fold 2   Fold 3   Fold 4

Stitch

Folds for headdress

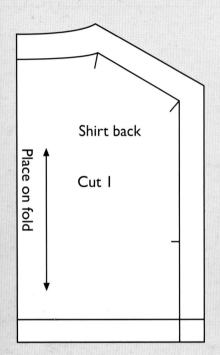

Shirt back

Place on fold

Cut 1

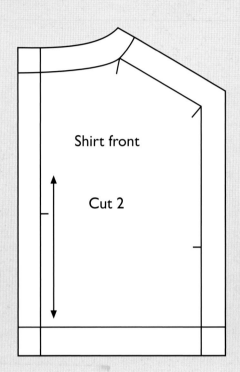

Shirt front

Cut 2

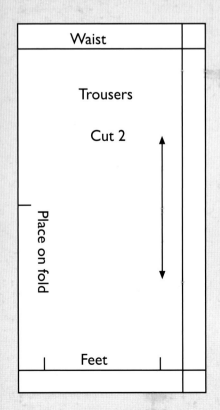

Waist

Trousers

Cut 2

Place on fold

Feet

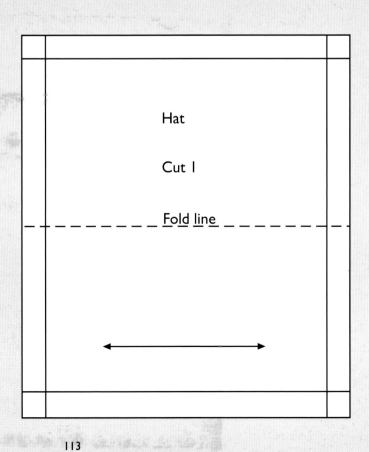

Hat

Cut 1

Fold line